Demystifying ~~ _usiness Strategy

In this book, David Lei and John W. Slocum offer readers a comprehensive overview of the drivers of *evolutionary advantage*, recognizing that sources of competitive advantage for any organization will necessarily shift and evolve in response to changes in the industry environment. *Demystifying Your Business Strategy* also offers practical insights on how to spot "inflection points" of strategic transition and identify signals that indicate when an organization needs to develop a new source of competitive advantage. With in-depth discussion of the four different types of business strategies that many firms pursue and the strategic disciplines that support them, this book can provide significant insight and direction to managers at all levels within an organization.

David Lei is Associate Professor of Strategy and Entrepreneurship at the Cox School of Business at Southern Methodist University, Dallas, Texas. His research has examined topics such as competitive strategy, strategic alliances, global strategy, and organizational issues. He has authored/co-authored over 40 articles and has consulted with numerous organizations (e.g., EDS, Texas Instruments, Corning, The Sabre Group, IBM, Fidelity Investments) on issues related to strategic planning and strategic renewal.

John W. Slocum is Professor Emeritus at the Cox School of Business at Southern Methodist University, Dallas, Texas. He has consulted for numerous organizations such as Aramark, Andrews Distributing Company, Kimberly Clark, AAA, Celanese, KeySpan Energy, University of North Texas Health Science Center, NASA, and OxyChem. A former President of the Academy of Management, he is the Associate Editor of *Organizational Dynamics*, *Journal of World Business*, and *Journal of Leadership & Organization Studies*. He has written 24 college management textbooks for Cengage Learning and is the author of *The Smarter Organization* (Wiley, 1994).

Demystifying Your Business Strategy

David Lei & John W. Slocum

Routledge
Taylor & Francis Group

NEW YORK AND LONDON

First published 2014
by Routledge
711 Third Avenue, New York, NY 10017

Simultaneously published in the UK
by Routledge
2 Park Square, Milton Park, Abingdon, Oxon OX14 4RN

Routledge is an imprint of the Taylor & Francis Group, an informa business

Library of Congress Cataloging in Publication Data
Lei, David.
Demystifying your business strategy/David Lei & John W. Slocum.
pages cm.
Includes bibliographical references and index.
1. Strategic planning.   I. Slocum, John W.   II. Title.
HD30.28.L4486 2013
658.4'012—dc23

2012049318

ISBN: 978–0–415–53866–4 (hbk)
ISBN: 978–0–415–53867–1 (pbk)
ISBN: 978–0–203–10900–7 (ebk)

Typeset in Adobe Caslon and Copperplate Gothic
by RefineCatch Limited, Bungay, Suffolk

Printed and bound in Great Britain by
TJ International Ltd, Padstow, Cornwall

TABLE OF CONTENTS

PREFACE

This book represents the culmination of our intense interest in how organizations grow, evolve, and confront the numerous opportunities and challenges that spring forth from their environment. Since we began our careers, there have been literally hundreds of strategy books published on diverse issues such as competitive dynamics, value creation, core competencies, corporate renewal, new business ventures, managing new technologies, innovation, global strategy, and corporate restructuring. At its core, strategy is all about an organization attaining distinction by providing a superior product or service in the eyes of its customer. This distinction needs to be a capability that outmaneuvers competitors along some key value-adding activity, or perhaps an organizational process that promotes and embraces innovation. Strategy is about making hard choices—which customers to serve, which approaches to take when entering new markets, how to achieve distinction in a service or product, and the timing or sequencing of key actions. These choices must be considered from an integrated perspective that allows senior executives to allocate precious resources according to what the organization can do best. By its very nature, strategy is forward-looking, but it is executed effectively only when the entire organization is aligned to support it.

Over the past several decades, we have enjoyed, and learned from the thousands of students, practicing managers and executives we have taught. It is to them that we dedicate this book. Throughout our teaching and research endeavors, we have remained intrigued by why some organizations have been able to prosper over long periods, even when their business environment seems to turn against them. Conversely, we find ourselves asking why so many organizations seem unable to adapt to their customers' changing needs, the advent of new technologies, or the development of new product ideas that plant the seeds from which new industries will emerge. Yet, we continue to feel optimistic about the inherent resourcefulness, industriousness, and initiative of entrepreneurs, and the spirit of enterprise, no matter where it emanates.

Ultimately, this book is about senior executives making strategic decisions that allow their organizations to develop and flourish. When we asked senior leaders about their biggest competitive advantage, most CEOs say that it is their ability to flawlessly execute their strategy. What is your firm's strategy? Is your firm a pioneer, consolidator, trend-setter or reinventor? By taking our strategy questionnaire, you will be able to determine the strategy that fits your organization best. Often, leaders are held back by their lack of focus. Many organizations find themselves floundering when they lack direction. It is the CEO and his/her leadership team's job to design not only a well thought-out mission, but also a solid strategy that will translate it into real actions and high performance. The leadership team is responsible for monitoring the success of their organization's strategy and for changing it if it is not effective. PIONEERS are successful when they compete in a dynamic or changing business world and can use their discipline of product leadership to drive their strategy; CONSOLIDATORS, on the other hand, are successful when they operate in a stable environment, can develop cost-efficient processes and supply chains, and apply their discipline of operational excellence to achieve superior results; TRENDSETTERS identify new or underserved market needs to create new value propositions and rely on their discipline of customer intimacy to satisfy evolving customer expectations; and finally REINVENTORS attempt to adapt to an increasingly dynamic business environment where their pre-existing offerings and core competencies face new types of external challenges. These organizations need to pursue a discipline of careful resource allocation by identifying and targeting markets for growth and renewal.

Our book is oriented towards professionals and executives and as a result, we chose to emphasize applications and examples rather than academic theory. You will probably be familiar with many of the organizations we cite in the book. Each chapter reviews what you can put in practice when thinking about and tackling issues related to crafting a successful business strategy. Examples are taken from a wide variety of industries to enhance the reader's comfort level. Each chapter concludes with a section explaining how you can understand and master the essentials of that chapter's topic.

In writing this book, we are indebted to many people for their constructive comments, suggestions, and ideas. The thousands of Executive MBAs at the Cox School who have endured our lectures and helped us frame our thinking are appreciated. We have often said that "Learning begins with the acknowledgement that you don't know," and we have learned a lot about crafting business strategies from our teaching and consulting engagements. We would like to thank Maribeth Kuenzi for her outstanding knowledge of statistics and research methodologies—both of which laid the foundation for the questionnaire instrument that is offered in this book. Carl Sewell's business acumen has been a constant source of inspiration to us. His largess and generosity to SMU, as well as that of O. Paul Corley and Ed Cox, have benefited our writing activities. Certainly, the intellectual prowess and contributions of legendary academic scholars Donald Hambrick and James Fredrickson have shaped the field of strategic management in profound and lasting ways. Their strategy model, developed in 2001, provides the backdrop for developing many of our ideas. To our editor, John Szilagyi, we owe an enormous debt of gratitude—for his friendship, his humor, his stewardship and guidance over this and many previous book projects, and for his personal encouragement, too! And, of course, no manuscript is ever complete without the extremely helpful administrative assistance from three great ladies who put up with us for so many years—Wanda Hanson, Jeanne Milazzo, and Jan Olavarri—all of the Cox School of Business at Southern Methodist University. We also sincerely appreciate all of the work put forth by the many dedicated people who proofread, copy-edited, and recommended numerous changes—all of which benefited our work enormously.

We would also like to thank and acknowledge the following individuals: Bill Joyce, Todd Diener, Barry Bales, Cindy Baker, Andy Kohlberg, Tom Fairchild, John Hammock, Sue Hammond, Mike Harvey, Don Hellriegel, Andrew Hiduke, Ellen Jackofsky, Chip Jarnagin, Jack Kennedy, Jake Sagehorn, Charlie Dana, Ellie Luce, Bill Reisel, Barry Mike, Wayne Wisniewski, Chuck Snow, Peter Heslin, Cindi Fitzgerald, Don Ritter, Chris Koski, Tom Corbin, Bill Detweiler, Dick Mason, Mike Beer, Jeff Sonnenfeld, Mick McGill, Ron Kirkpatrick, Don Tuttle, Ralph Sorrentino, Mike McGuire, Jim Ruth, and Mark Gilbert. We want to thank too the leadership teams at Andrews Distributing Company, Kisco Senior Living Communities, ViewCast Corporation, and the University of North Texas Health Science Center for helping us develop our questionnaire and the hundreds of executives who pretested the questionnaire and gave us constructive feedback.

David Lei
Dallas, Texas
John W. Slocum
Dallas, Texas

1

CRAFTING A SUSTAINABLE
BUSINESS STRATEGY

Consider the strategic situation confronting these companies today:

Best Buy, a leading U.S. retailer of consumer electronics, computers, flat-screen televisions, and household appliances has grown phenomenally over the last ten years, vanquishing its big-box competition in every major market. Yet, this same retailer now faces a possible death sentence as a result of the way it does business. Increasingly, customers visit the stores not so much with the intention to buy, but to capture product identification bar codes that will guide them to the least expensive provider through their digital smartphones. Best Buy is becoming less of a "retailer" and more of a "showroom," thus exposing major weaknesses in its once formidable business model. These unforeseen changes have also forced major changes in top leadership, including the resignation in 2012 of Best Buy's CEO, Brian Dunn.

A leading-edge player in the semiconductor industry, Qualcomm has always been at the forefront of the microchips used in cell phones, digital networks, and even Apple's iPad line of appliances. By helping set the standards for how data is compressed and transmitted over wireless spectra, Qualcomm has laid the foundation for continued future growth through continuous innovation and fierce protection of its intellectual property in the wake of ambitious smaller companies seeking to catch up.

One upstart bio-tech firm is working on cutting-edge cancer research and devising new gene-based therapies designed to treat each individual patient's ailments through customized treatments that avoid much of the collateral cell damage and side effects of traditional, one-size-fits-all therapies. Yet, in its quest to grow, it is facing a number of critical business challenges, including raising cash, navigating the regulatory approval process, and the ever-present threat that better-funded larger companies may beat it to the punch in product development.

Sara Lee, a giant in the food-processing industry, is facing a wave of competitive challenges as its well-known brands and products face severe pricing pressure from other large food companies and private-label producers. Although American consumers love Sara Lee's pound cake, Hillshire Farms meats and other brands, major grocery retailers are squeezing the firm's profits as the industry's growth rate slows to a crawl and consumers themselves feel squeezed as incomes stagnate. Seeking to protect its profit sanctuaries, Sara Lee is outsourcing non-core brands and operations and attempting to streamline its internal processes in order to yield rising efficiencies in an increasingly brutal market. At the end of 2012, Sara Lee completely divested itself of all its non-food brands and changed its name to Hillshire Farms.

There is little doubt that firms and organizations of all sizes face a growing variety of challenges—a "flatter world" of intense competition, ever-demanding customers, rapid technological change, and perhaps most important, business practices that don't seem robust enough to sustain competitive advantage over long periods. Although everyone in business knows how difficult it is to raise capital, find and serve knowledgeable customers, select and develop the right talented staff, and improve operations, it seems as though even those companies described as "most admired," "the best to work for," or at the top of any business magazine list are just as vulnerable as anyone else to downturns. The industrial graveyard is littered with once-great industry icons as corporate titanics collide with economic icebergs when these firms navigate unknown waters. From an earlier era, RCA, Westinghouse Electric, K-Mart, Montgomery Ward, Ampex, Timex, and Memorex (to name just a few) have either slipped off the edges of a hotter, flatter world, or faded into mere shadows of their former selves. This past decade alone, once-darling U.S. firms such as Circuit City, Borders, Filene's Basement, Blockbuster, General Motors, MCI WorldCom, Sears, and Tyco have either disappeared, entered bankruptcy, restructured, or become so irrelevant to their customers that their names hardly elicit a yawn. Yesterday's winners often morph into tomorrow's dinosaurs. Seemingly, organizations continue to grow and expand until they reach the point of maximum vulnerability. Corporate paragons in one era serve as corpses for business school students to dissect a few years later.

Vulnerability to change remains a part of doing business—it is part of an organization's DNA. Remaining vibrant and competitive presents a permanent challenge to stay fresh and relevant, and to remain true to what one does best. Vulnerability exists throughout a business's exist-ence, from the time it is born to when it grows, matures, and adapts to its environment. Every organization is at one point unique—it has founders who believe that they can create something great. Yet, at its core, each business begins and evolves with an individual "gene code" based on its customers (who it will serve), its processes (how it will create value to serve them), its leaders (their priorities, focus, dedication to the business), its staff (who it hires, develops, retains), and most important, its vision—the reason and purpose for its existence every day. This "gene code" means that each organization will have its own unique set of priorities, strengths and weaknesses as it grows and adapts. For example, businesses dedicated to serving the wealthy customer, such as Neiman-Marcus, Tiffany & Co., and Ritz-Carlton, face a very different set of considerations and vulnerabilities than those focused on the middle class or the economically pinched, such as Kohl's, Dillard's, or Best Western. The former businesses' "gene code" may be more suscep-tible to changes in upper-income marginal tax rates, while rising gas prices impact the latter businesses' prospects. Likewise, a high-tech firm that sets the standard for cutting-edge product breakthroughs and designs faces a different vulnerability than a mass-producer of low-cost standardized products. Patent protection and branding image are big considerations for Apple, while cost-containment and outsourcing are important to Vizio and Hitachi.

Setting a Strategic Vision

All C-level managers know that a clear strategic vision is requisite for their company's ability to compete in today's globally competitive world. At Sears, K-Mart, Blockbuster, Eastman Kodak, and others, strategic vision vacillated between trying to introduce new products to meet today's market and focusing on their ability to execute these visions. Failing companies do not possess the necessary capabilities for developing or pursuing bold new strategies that deviate from their clouded view of what they could be. Over time, it became clear for these firms that product proliferation and entry into too many new markets was neither optimizing revenues from existing customers, nor attracting new customers. One of the most important decisions for managers is to understand how closely these new imperatives (products, markets) align themselves with their organization's vision.

The foundation of any business rests on a strategic vision, that revolves around key existential tenets such as "What does the organization want to be?" "Who do we want to serve?" These are not merely rhetorical questions, but help firms choose a lifelong direction and act as a guidepost for being. A strategic vision casts an organization's *identity and purpose*. The best strategic visions are clear, simple, and understandable by everyone in the organization. Consider, for example, these powerful visions:

- Southwest Airlines—fun, low fares;
- Coca-Cola—a Coke within an arm's reach;
- General Electric—Number One or Number Two in what we do;
- CNN—24-hour news;
- Sewell Automotive—customers for life;
- Hyundai Motor—a race to the top.

When one thinks about Southwest Airlines, one can't help but notice the friendly service, dedication of its employees, a "can-do" attitude, and the fast turnaround of its planes. Southwest takes only twenty minutes to unload its passengers, clean and restock its aircraft, and help its next customers board before flying on to another destination. Along the way, customers are delighted with the welcoming smiles and helpful service that define the way pilots and flight attendants treat passengers—in sharp contrast with other major airlines beset with entrenched labor problems (e.g., American Airlines). Yet, the unique character and special feel of Southwest Airlines is due in large part to former CEO Herb Kelleher and people leader Colleen Barrett, both of whom crafted and promoted Southwest's fun-oriented culture. The firm's vision is stunningly simple—offer low fares and make flying fun. For a considerable period, Kelleher personally embodied and lived this Southwest way of flying. One day a week, Kelleher would work as a flight attendant and serve drinks and peanuts to happy passengers on full planes, all the while telling bad jokes and making fun of himself. Much larger rivals, such as American, Delta, US Airways and United/Continental, all feared "the Southwest effect." Any airport that Southwest chose to serve eventually saw one or more competitors being crushed and often their subsequent exit.

Perhaps the most enduring legacy of Jack Welch's eighteen years as CEO of General Electric was the renewed focus and discipline that his leadership team instilled throughout this firm. Having assumed the CEO post in 1982, Welch quickly found pockets of inefficiency and slow-growth/dying businesses throughout GE, including those related to television sets, oil-drilling equipment, factory equipment, small motors, and home appliances. Welch and his team began a long journey of revitalizing General Electric through a very simple strategic vision: Be Number One or Number Two, or face the prospect of being sold. Over the next ten years, GE slimmed down its bloated bureaucracy, sliced through layers of superfluous management, sold off dozens of less profitable businesses, and acquired fast-growing companies to build a strong market position in each GE business unit that dominated its market. Known as "Neutron Jack" because of GE's massive downsizing, Welch also insisted that GE managers reached for the stars in their own career paths. GE managers learned the ins-and-outs of financial discipline, operational excellence, and Six Sigma techniques that yielded enormous gains in productivity while simultaneously eliminating waste throughout the organization.

Coca-Cola has been around for over a hundred years. It has faced numerous challenges, including tough competition from the likes of PepsiCo and Dr Pepper/Snapple. Yet, the basics of Coke's enduring strategy remain its unwavering focus on operational excellence and reinforcing its numerous distribution channels. "A Coke within an arm's reach" has long provided the vision that guides strategy and entry into new markets worldwide. Coke's investments range from bottling plants and vending machines to equity stakes in beverage distributors in major markets. Yet, when Coke deviated from its operations-driven strategy, it suffered setbacks. During the 1980s, Coke toyed around with entering the winery business, and even owned half of Columbia Pictures before it was subsequently sold to Sony in 1989. Neither viniculture nor movie-making fit with Coke's defining strategic vision.

Dallas-based Sewell Automotive is extremely well respected among its competitors for delivering the highest possible standards of customer service in the automobile retailing industry. Founded more than a century ago, in its earliest days the firm even assembled automobiles from kits before selling them to customers. Now, Sewell is synonymous with dedicated customer loyalty—in many cases, lasting through a customer's (and his/her family's) lifetime. Customer service runs deep in Sewell's DNA—so deep that the company will do almost anything to help a customer with his/her automotive buying and repair needs. In his book *Customers for Life*, CEO Carl Sewell describes succinctly the simple and yet powerful steps that any organization can take to build a profitable business through a laser-like, galvanized dedication to serving each customer.

Thirty years ago, cars from Hyundai Motor were joked about on late-night television and throughout the automobile industry. The first Hyundai Excels arrived in the United States in 1985 and found few buyers, except perhaps from Korean-American customers who were proud of the fact that South Korea had finally transformed itself into an advanced industrial economy. Yet, disappointing sales and poor initial quality did not deter this dedicated company from seeking to emulate and even beat rival Toyota. Beating the Japanese became a mantra throughout Hyundai. The company left no stone unturned in its search for ways to dramatically improve its cars' quality, performance, comfort, fuel economy and safety. Hyundai redoubled its efforts to serve its small but growing U.S. market by offering an unprecedented ten-year, 100K mile warranty on its cars. This generous policy helped assuage many lingering concerns among customers. Behind the scenes, Hyundai invested heavily in electronics, plastics, engineering materials, and advanced engines to catch up with its Japanese rivals. Hyundai knew that without earning respect and market share in the U.S. market, it could not win customers anywhere else around the world. Hyundai's extreme dedication to improving its product durability and quality finally thrust several of its models onto the cover pages of such magazines as *Consumer Reports* and *Car and Driver*, where it has begun to win over important critical reviews.

Shaping the Future

A strategic vision sets the direction and the tone for the entire organization. It drives how the business organizes its activities and processes; develops and measures its people; and prioritizes its investments for future growth. When charting its growth, an organization finds guidance from its strategic vision. Clear vision prioritizes what the business must do when it faces new and unanticipated competitive challenges and threats. Figure 1.1 provides a roadmap that shows how a vision guides the business' development of its key activities.

Many people will argue that a strategic vision should represent something very abstract, noble, uplifting, or even romantic in its quest. We agree with that premise. Some of our aforementioned examples have exceptionally lofty and yet simple visions, such as "customers for life" at Sewell Automotive, or "fun and low fares" at Southwest Airlines. Other powerful visions can be overtly competitive and directed, as we can see in Hyundai Motor's strivings to be Number One, or General Electric's aim of being Number One or Number Two. Every organization needs a strategic vision, and at a minimum it should be crystal clear to all stakeholders. Figure 1.1 lays out the basis for any

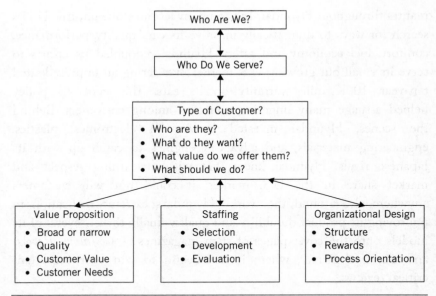

Figure 1.1 The Foundation of a Strategic Vision.

organization's strategic vision in stark business terms from the lofty to the operational. It all begins with the most basic of all questions: "WHO ARE WE?"

Who Are We?
This simple question gets right to the point: Why are you in business? Can you do something valuable that no one else has succeeded? This question also presents in stark brutal relief what you can and can't do. Senior executives need to know their organization's strengths and weaknesses before they undertake something. Do you have something to prove? Did you overcome a horrible past experience that gives you the galvanized focus and unrelenting energy to compete in some way? Merely thinking about these questions can present important opportunities for self-discovery. Southwest knew that it could not become a nationwide airline overnight—it was too much of a stretch for a start-up with little capital operating in three Texas cities, despite the magnetic and overwhelming energy of its founding leaders. Hyundai

Motor knew that entering the U.S. market would be a long-term endeavor—a journey that would take decades. Can its management team and its people withstand the rigors of competing with the Japanese long-term? As the ancient Chinese strategist Sun Tzu once remarked some two millennia ago, you have to know yourself (and your rivals) to win a hundred battles.

Who Do We Serve?
This is the most important question that defines the underlying scope of a business. "Who do we serve" means much more than who should we target as customers: the question opens up the entire panoply of issues related to strategy, customers, the value proposition, the staffing of the business, and the key operational processes to keep things running. Answering this question acts as a starting point for designing and constructing the essential linchpins of the entire organization. For example, Procter & Gamble's "Swiffer®" product line is a case in point. P&G deployed a cadre of seventy senior employees around the world to help identify new product opportunities that would serve customers in both developed and emerging markets. These "technology entrepreneurs" are responsible for researching a variety of sources. In many instances, they also observe in person how customers utilize P&G products in order to find new offerings that build upon the firm's core business. From these entrepreneurs, the new Swiffer® line was created as P&G knew that the long-handled mop was still the primary product used to clean floors. It drew on the ideas of its advisory team, and also listened to its customers, to create this new product range and grow an entirely new category.

The beginning and end of any business is the customer. Businesses prosper only to the extent that they can design and provide products and services that customers are willing to pay for. It is obvious that customers are the lifeblood of each and every business, but it is a lesson that is all too often forgotten, especially when businesses grow and forget their origins. Thinking like the customer, anticipating his/her needs, and providing a perfect product or service are the fundamental building blocks of success.

Type of Customer?

An old Roman adage once stated that: "A ship without direction will find no wind favorable." Or, as numerous literary works have commented: "One cannot be all things to all people." Businesses need to precisely target and serve the type of customer they will serve. The choice of customer type, in turn, will set the stage for what their needs are. Determining what a customer wants is tricky business: large-scale surveys, demographic studies, and marketing research programs offer only a limited explanation. These rough measures provide a profile for some "average" customer with "average" needs; interesting, but hardly the sole basis for committing valuable resources to a business endeavor.

Who are They?

Do I know who I want to serve? Do I understand what they do, how they live, how they are likely to use my organization's product or service? Do I have a gut-feeling for what they truly value?

Value Offered?

Understanding the type of customer you want to serve and his/her needs leads to an equally important question: What do they value and can we offer it? As a business, why should anyone come to me, rather than my competitor who is more likely to be established, better known, and probably better situated to serve him/her? What kind of value can I offer my customer that others cannot do so as well as me?

What Should We Do?

This question relates to the fundamentals of setting up and running a business. Obviously, financing is the first thing that comes to most people's minds. One can't do anything without cash: you can't hire people, design your products, test them in the marketplace, advertise or market them, and pay all the necessary legal and regulatory expenses. Beyond cash, there are some absolutely core issues that impact both the start-up as well as the established organization—these issues remain omnipresent and reflect the firm's strategic vision.

Value Propositions

A value proposition is the set of products or services that the business offers to its customers at a price where it can make a profit. In practice, a value proposition can be as simple as lemonade offered for fifty cents on a street stand, or as complex as software integration solutions offered by high-tech firms such as SAP, Oracle, or Microsoft. Regardless, designing the value proposition compels the firm to think hard about many issues, including the "four Ps" of marketing: product, pricing, positioning, and promotion.

Broad or Narrow?

Does the business want to offer a single product, a limited range of similar/related products, or expand to include a variety of different products? Also, how will the firm go about creating, producing and delivering the product? Should the firm undertake all of these steps by itself, or outsource some—or even all—aspects of this activity?

Quality

Quality has become a given in any business. Each and every customer expects to receive a perfect product or perfectly executed service each time they pay for it. Yet, a race to achieve ever higher levels of quality remains an important competitive weapon for firms seeking to distinguish themselves from their rivals. For many businesses, a perfect product or service is just the beginning of a marathon whose purpose is to capture lifelong, loyal customers.

Customer Value

Clearly this dimension directly relates to the type of customer the business seeks to serve. Pricing is an important dimension of customer value, but not exclusively. Customer value also refers to what he/she wants in terms of how the product or service offers satisfaction along a variety of measures. These can include superior benefits, fewer costs of aggravation (e.g., ease of maintenance, easy of installation or upgrades, compatibility with other products, availability anytime anywhere).

Of course, the number of competitors in the market constrains what a business can charge. Likewise, customers' perception of value is likely to change significantly as the product's availability becomes more widespread, or when the product's features become standardized to the point that it is hard to distinguish one firm's offerings from another's.

Customer Needs

How does the organization aim to satisfy its customers' current and future needs? Will the business seek to adapt its products according to what its current customers desire, or will the business seek to anticipate what needs might arise? How will the business attract future customers to its products and services? Will current customers remain loyal to its offerings? What other organizations or firms can become potent competitors in meeting customers' needs? What ground should the business stake out for its products and services?

Staffing

Constructing a robust and competitive organization requires many building blocks and vital decisions must be made about such issues as choice of structure, systems, staffing, etc. We believe the paramount ingredient is staffing the business. Selecting, developing, and retaining the right people are essential to a business's long-term health and viability. If an organization is unable to attract the requisite talent and skills, it might as well give up and go home. Talent is needed at every level in any organization—and the most critical jobs are not necessarily the highest-level ones. At its core, staffing encompasses three vital focal points: selection, development, and evaluation.

Selection

Attracting those individuals with the best fitting skills to fill critical jobs is enormously important. Ideally, hiring should involve taking a longer-term view: the organization should assess to what extent today's skills will need to change as the business evolves. Sometimes an individual who has the perfect skill set for today's critical job may fall short of what is needed for tomorrow. This leads to the second focal point: development.

Development

Skill requirements for critical jobs will become more demanding as competitive pressures ramp up and new technologies proliferate. One can never assume that a successful person will succeed in a different job or when he/she is promoted. It is often the case that a highly experienced person can deliver outstanding performance in one job, but is unable to deliver when transferred or promoted to another position. Development enables people to receive training and skill upgrades that sustain their ability to contribute.

Evaluation

An organization cannot know if it has attained the best match between talent and job requirements without periodically evaluating the fit.

Organization Design

Every organization or business is actually the sum of all the internal systems in place. Everything must work in tandem to ensure that customers receive the value they pay for. This synchronicity of a business' activities to produce value is known as a "process."

Processes are found everywhere in any business; some of the better known ones include supply chain and accounting, order fulfillment, quality control, and billing. The most important thing about any given process is that it should support the organization's vision and strategy. The best designed processes are those that do things right at the outset.

As the business evolves, so too must its processes. Some organizations benchmark their processes and standards against those with leading-edge best practices. However, time stands still for no one. Continuous, relentless process improvement can dramatically improve total business performance for any firm in any industry, as practiced by many Japanese automotive manufacturers, U.S. semiconductor firms, and leading hotel chains around the world.

Mastering the Essentials of Crafting a Strategy

Mastering the essentials of crafting a strategy involves:

- identifying a customer need;
- creating a strategic vision;
- crafting your value proposition;
- attracting and retaining key talent.

2

TRANSLATING A VISION
INTO STRATEGY

Transforming a vision into concrete results demands that an organization has a clear strategy for success. But what exactly is strategy? Over the past three decades, there have been literally dozens of conceptions of strategy, including such well-known phrases as core competencies, co-alignment, value creation, value chains, industry analysis, breakthrough thinking, pursuit of excellence, knowledge management, execution, winning, and prioritizing. The list could go on and on.

At its heart, *strategy* is a coherent set of integrated choices about what an organization will do in order to accomplish its goals and objectives. *Integrated choices* refer to the fact that there are many functions and avenues related to managing the business—for example, how will we enter a market, which customers to serve, how will we create the product/service, which technologies to invest in, how do we grow over time. How a business decides to answer one question has a direct impact on the others. This view of strategy compels C-level executives to think deeply and systematically about how all of the pieces fit together.

Successful firms are like psalms: their choices and parts fit together harmoniously by focusing on a particular approach or way to offer customers compelling value. Organizations build competitive advantage when they take actions that enable them to gain an edge over their rivals in some key way of doing business.

By its very nature, strategy is also about *tradeoffs*—what an organization will choose to do and not to do. For example, by choosing to serve the mass market, we will probably limit our appeal to upper and lower income extremes; or by choosing to be the technology leader, we will have to invest proportionately more in product research than a firm who chooses to be a late adopter. The choice of tradeoffs ultimately guides and constrains the business' short- and medium-term actions. Failure to recognize tradeoffs results in a "mission fog" by which the business does not distinguish itself in any way from its competitors and eventually dies.

Professor Michael Porter of the Harvard Business School elaborated on the notion of competitive advantage in his seminal works over the past three decades. He points out that strategy is not the same thing as attaining operational excellence or becoming an efficiently managed organization. Processes such as the just-in-time inventory management systems or Six Sigma quality improvement techniques, as practiced by Motorola and General Electric, represent major corporate endeavors to rejuvenate businesses. These are not strategies in their own right. In other words, attaining higher levels of operational efficiencies and increased productivity are worthy steps, but they are not synonymous with strategy.[1]

Strategy sets the direction for the rest of the organization to support it. Selecting a given strategy in turn provides the basis for determining how critical organizational systems support and buttress the strategy. These organizational systems can include the type of reporting structure used, performance and evaluation systems that measure outcomes, career paths, and the design of processes that create and deliver value to customers. Senior managers should consider effective organization design as a vital part of the strategy-making process, but not a substitute for it.

It is useful at this stage to highlight the key difference between corporate-level strategy and business-level strategy, since managers sometimes use these terms interchangeably. In essence, corporate-level strategy deals with the boundaries of the firm: it addresses the broader issue of "which businesses should the firm be in?" As such, corporate-level strategy should *not* be the sum of all of the company's parts, but rather add value above and beyond that generated at the business level. If the firm's corporate strategy cannot do this, the businesses are better off left standing alone.

Business-level strategy deals with the question of "how do we compete in a given market?" Will the firm compete on cost, quality, after-sales service, product features, etc.? It is more specific and should be based on a set of priorities and steps needed to create competitive advantage. Competitive advantage represents an edge that an organization has over its competitors.

At this point, it is worthy to ask the reader to think about his/her business. There are many different drivers of business strategy, some more important than others. While there is no doubt that the economic environment surrounding a business is important, managers have significant discretion to choose how they want their business to compete. We offer a short questionnaire to allow the reader to obtain a general profile of what kinds of strategic considerations are likely to become especially relevant in the way he/she thinks about his/her business' future.

Our questionnaire is designed to give you a concise, succinct overview of the most important strategic drivers of your business.[2] Based on the responses you provide, the scores indicate the degree to which you believe your business predominantly fits into one of four very broad categories. These four categories are 1) consolidator, 2) pioneer, 3) trendsetter, and 4) reinventor. Let us now briefly consider what these terms mean as they relate to your business.

The following questions are designed to help you evaluate your organization's business strategy. Please complete the following 20 questions using the scale provided.

	Completely false	Disagree	Neutral	Agree	Very true
1. We outsource key business activities to minimize costs.	1	2	3	4	5
2. We seek to standardize our offerings to our customers.	1	2	3	4	5
3. It is essential to work with our suppliers to minimize costs.	1	2	3	4	5
4. Cost reduction is our unit's number one day-to-day focus.	1	2	3	4	5
5. Dynamic product innovation is rare in our industry.	1	2	3	4	5
6. We strive to produce a continuous stream of state-of-the-art products/services.	1	2	3	4	5
7. Creativity in conceiving new product or marketing ideas is highly prized and rewarded in our business.	1	2	3	4	5
8. Our business is active in pursuing new product ideas and solutions to customer problems.	1	2	3	4	5
9. Our business unit's CEO likes to think out of the box.	1	2	3	4	5
10. Our CEO has a marketing background.	1	2	3	4	5
11. Our ability to roll out new products represents a major business strength.	1	2	3	4	5
12. Exceeding customers' expectations is the foundation of our existence.	1	2	3	4	5
13. Product lines are very broad compared to competitors.	1	2	3	4	5
14. Retaining our most creative marketing people is essential to continued business success.	1	2	3	4	5
15. Allocating resources between product lines is extremely important.	1	2	3	4	5
16. Our dominant business is mature although we have products in faster growing dynamic markets.	1	2	3	4	5
17. In our industry, we have witnessed disruptions because of new technologies.	1	2	3	4	5
18. Cash flow requirements among business units result in interdepartmental/unit conflicts.	1	2	3	4	5
19. Seeking external sources of financing for new product ideas or technology is vital to our success.	1	2	3	4	5
20. Our business unit consumes more cash than it generates.	1	2	3	4	5

Scoring: Add questions 1–5   Total _____. This is your Consolidator score.
            Add questions 6–10   Total _____. This is your Pioneer score.
            Add questions 11–15   Total _____. This is your Trendsetter score.
            Add questions 16–20   Total _____. This is your Reinventor score.

- If your total score for questions 1–5 is more than that of any other category, you are a Consolidator.
- If your total score for questions 6–10 is more than that of any other category, you are a Pioneer.
- If your total score for questions 11–15 is more than that of any other category, you are a Trendsetter.
- If your total score for questions 16–20 is more than that of any other category, you are a Reinventor.

Consolidators face great pressure to streamline their business and to achieve cost reductions across all functions. Business profitability is synonymous with leanness and cost efficiency. This is the hallmark of competing in a mature market. A major priority for consolidators is to undertake decisions that reinforce their capability to compete on cost. A consolidator's cost-driven focus leads it to look for opportunities to standardize its operations as well as its product offerings to its customers. Examples of consolidators include Wal-Mart Stores, Carrefour, Royal Ahold NV, Flextronics, Akzo-Nobel, Grupo Bimbo, Mabe, Taiwan Semiconductor Manufacturing, Hon-Hai Precision Manufacturing Company (a.k.a. Foxconn), Amazon.com, Briggs & Stratton, and the like.

Pioneers seek to create an entirely new way of serving your customers through bold, cutting-edge products that lay the foundation for enormous growth and profitability in the future. Because they seek to chart a completely new path, pioneers—such as the online clothing and shoe store Zappos.com, the social games company Zynga, and the diabetes drug researcher Amilyn Pharmaceuticals—ultimately create products and services that in turn become new industries in their own right. Pioneers typically populate young, high-growth industries where barriers to entry are low, innovation rates high, demand hard to predict, and firms' competitive positions in flux.

Trendsetters find themselves competing against other businesses in an environment where product innovation and capturing customer loyalty drive competitive advantage. Often, a business seeks to set and raise the standards (e.g., product features, novelty, technical soundness) for what their customers should expect and how their rivals will compete. Trendsetters thrive on building customer intimacy that earns them repeat business time and again; Sewell Automotive, Brinker International, Dyson, LVMH Moet-Hennessy Louis Vuitton, Hermes, Harley-Davidson, Apple, and Andrews Distributing Company all shape customer expectations of what kind of value they should pay for.

In many situations, a firm's products face rapid obsolescence and growing competition from rivals who have completely changed the basis of how products and services are created and valued by customers.

Businesses confronting this strategic setting need to reinvent the way they do business. **Reinventors**, such as Texas Instruments, General Dynamics, United Technologies, and Barnes & Noble, face the challenging task of allocating resources away from their existing products to create faster-growing new products.

In the chapters that follow (Chapters 4 through 7), we will highlight and analyze the critical success factors needed for each of these strategy types—consolidator, pioneer, trendsetter, and reinventor—to succeed.

Finding the Right Strategy

The choice of strategies that suit one particular business well may not translate into competitive advantage or success for another. It is simply impossible to delineate a universal set of strategic principles that apply to all firms. There are scores, if not hundreds, of industries that define and drive today's economic life. As a firm's environment changes, so will many of the drivers that senior management must consider when utilizing their capabilities to compete and navigate the firm through a changing economic landscape. Likewise, managers' choices and actions also directly impact strategy. A great strategic plan is meaningless if it is not executed successfully. Managers must take steps to ensure that the choice of their strategy coaligns with the rest of the organization. This means that formulating a strategy is just the first step of a larger, "big picture" endeavor that must also include other decisions, such as building the necessary strategic capabilities and disciplines to execute. What senior management may consider a very pressing issue in one industry (e.g., patent protection for drugs or video games) may be quite different in another (e.g., availability of low-cost steel in the construction and automotive industries).

Designing and implementing an effective business strategy is the hallmark of competitive advantage. An effective business strategy, in turn, requires the manager to be aware of not only the business' external environment, but also the critical success factors within the organization that impact the execution of that strategy. In sum, we can present a map to help managers think about how best to formulate and execute their strategies. Here are the "big picture" guidelines:

- the relative importance of the external environment facing the business;
- the design of a comprehensive strategic framework in which all the pieces of the strategy puzzle fit together.

We will consider each of these broad topics in detail. Let us begin by first examining the external environment facing the business, as illustrated in Figure 2.1.

The External Environment

Regardless of the product or service offered, every organization must adapt to a changing, external environment. Customer needs, revised product designs, technological breakthroughs, new process improvements, and competitors' actions represent just a few of the major drivers of change in the business environment. When organizations ignore them, they do so at great peril. Witness the current troubles plaguing *The New York Times*, *The Chicago Tribune*, the *Los Angeles Times*, and the entire daily U.S. newspaper industry as it grapples with delivering information in a tablet computer or smartphone era. A hard-won

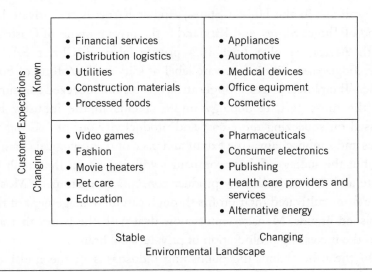

Figure 2.1 Broad Mapping of Industry Environments.

competitive advantage can face rapid obsolescence in the wake of these changes. In the worst situations, an organization's entire vision, strategy and business model can become completely irrelevant almost overnight. Let's examine how the external environment directly influences how senior management conceives strategy.

Strategy generally begins with an assessment of your industry. We believe that many factors come into play when C-level executives formulate their firm's strategy. As an industry evolves, customer expectations tend to become clearer (more known), and the environmental landscape becomes more stable, as shown in Figure 2.1. Conversely, there will be times in an industry when customer expectations change and the environmental landscape becomes unstable. This is usually the result of some type of external upheaval (e.g., new product technology, new competitors, government regulations, etc.).

In 2012, the food processing industry was relatively stable as it tends to grow only as fast as the population. Firms usually compete through product line extensions and customers know what they want to buy and how much they want to pay. One of the more significant challenges facing such major firms as ConAgra, H. J. Heinz, Kraft Foods, Kellogg and General Mills in the United States is the rise of private-label brands. For example, in the United States, Archer Farms is the private label brand of Target Stores, and Kirkland is the private brand of Costco. In South Africa, Tropika Juice is a private label of Clover SA, and Townlodges and City is a private label of City Lodge/Hotel of South Africa. Their lower prices strongly attract recession-squeezed consumers. For the most part, technology improvements in the industry have focused on squeezing more cost and productivity out of existing factories and supply chains. The extent and pace of technological change is low, but the success of these companies will depend on their ability to create and deliver fresh new product concepts to customers. Most of these firms cultivated their profits through careful management of their cherished brands. Managers must now deal with the issues that arise from the increasing proliferation of private-label brands.

On the other hand, the publishing industry is in the midst of a complete makeover. The rise of new types of digital information technologies have completely upended the way that book, newspaper, and magazine companies deliver their product to their customers, compete with one another, and gain access to new markets. The rise and immediate prevalence of game-changing new technologies have brought this industry to the brink. Traditional distribution facilities and channels, such as newspaper plants, book binderies, and even retail store locations, have become increasingly irrelevant to how businesses create and offer their products. Firms like textbook publisher Houghton Mifflin Harcourt, Pearson PLC, McGraw-Hill, and Cengage face significant financial difficulties as their brick-and-mortar cost structures and printing equipment become huge obstacles to attaining profitability in a digital publishing and transmission age. Students increasingly rent their textbooks through websites, and professors have become accustomed to creating their own customized course "packets" that often bypass formal textbooks. In 2012, Encyclopedia Britannica announced that its products will no longer appear in print form, thus exiting a traditional activity that lasted more than 200 years. Likewise, such stalwart news media firms as Gannett and Belo are steadily losing readers who look to websites for information.

The Progression of Time—Customer Expectations and Life Cycle Dynamics

Studying and understanding the dynamics of the product life cycle helps managers to grapple with the nature of how an industry evolves. Products evolve through the stages of introduction, growth, maturity, and decline at their own industry-specific rate. These stages also exert a direct bearing on how customer expectations tend to migrate over time. Each stage of the product life cycle generates its own set of strategic and organizational requirements, and thus requires a different "lens" and "set of tools" to monitor and deal with competitors.

The early stage of the life cycle, characterized by rapid growth, prolif-eration of product designs, and low barriers to entry, witnesses many firms' attempts to get their innovative products to market and accepted by customers. As the overall size of the market expands, it attracts a large number of competitors. This growth provides considerable economic ferment that is evident by the many creative ways that firms attempt to reach customers, whose needs are often unclear and fast-changing.

As the industry becomes mature, a dominant industry-wide approach of method to creating products and services becomes established. As a result, products tend to standardize over time, and markets saturate. Equally important, customers become smarter and know what they want, which makes it difficult for firms to raise prices. Declining differences generally lead to similar pricing and price-cutting. At this stage, firms become highly specialized and cost efficiency becomes important in determining profitability. Thus, the evolution of products and processes in most industries tends to exhibit strong life cycle characteristics. Recent examples of industries that have undergone such a progression include food processing, consumer electronics, and retailing.

Consider the fax machine. Until the past decade, the industry grew every year since 1970. Even though AT&T's legendary Bell Laboratories conceived the original idea, Xerox made the first commercial breakthrough with a portable fax that sold for $12,500, primarily to sales people. The early fax machine contained mechanical rather than electronic circuitry, and offered few features. From 1986 to 1998, the number of companies selling fax machines blossomed from one to 25, including such well-known names as IBM, Ricoh, Sharp, Toshiba, along with early standout Xerox. As a result of competitor entry and aggressive pricing, the average price plummeted from $3,500 in 1985 to $500 in 1995. Product features also increased dramatically, including such capabilities as color printing. Currently, fax machine capabilities face enormous competition from e-mail and other digital transmission technologies, and they are incorporated as part of a larger, multi-functional machine that includes scanning, copying and color reproduction. There are also a variety of small multi-functional machines aimed specifically at small business users as well as homeowners. Today, five manufacturers (Hewlett-Packard, Brother, Sharp, Lexmark and Samsung) account for over 90 per cent of sales and many of their machines sell for under $100. More than 120 billion faxes are sent annually.

Innovation and Changing the Rules of the Game

It has become all too commonplace to say we live in the world of change. Despite this hackneyed phrase, every firm in every industry feels the need to continue to improve what they do, from the offerings they design and sell, to the processes used to create value, the logistics of getting value to the customer, and the amount of time needed to do new things. Getting an idea commercialized into an economic valuable product or service is the defining principle of innovation.

Over the past ten years, there have been numerous studies examining the types of innovation that can impact how industries change. In our opinion, one of the most powerful and useful characterizations of innovation comes from the work of Clayton Christensen, who described two broad types: sustaining innovations and disruptive innovations.[3]

Few Business Upheavals—Stable Environmental Landscape

Many changes in an industry are gradual and occur in a way that both firms and customers can predict, as illustrated in Figure 2.1. Products and technologies follow a seemingly well defined, almost logical progression and trajectory. Sustaining innovations provide steady, incremental, measurable improvement. Each subsequent generation of new products incorporates improved features or functionality over the previous one, as we read about in the fax machine industry. Predictability of product planning and customer demand is high. The underlying core product technology remains stable for a long period of time. Thus, there is comparatively little uncertainty facing the firm when it designs a new product, since it tends to follow the same "design logic" of previous generations. When they do occur, technological or customer-driven breakthroughs are not sustaining innovations.

All firms engage in sustaining innovations to improve their offerings over time. Firms compete through continuous improvement of their products and processes. They search for new steps and practices that improve how a product feels or functions, operational efficiency, factory yield, cost improvement, supply chain responsiveness, or the incorporation of new attributes into an existing product design. Because sustaining innovations follow a seemingly predictable path, they give firms the impression that there are few real breakthroughs to transform how the product is designed or to dramatically redefine how to offer value to the customer. The hallmark of sustaining innovations is the notion of product and process refinement.

From a strategic perspective, organizations tend to mimic one another when undertaking sustaining innovations to improve their customer offerings. This makes it difficult to utilize sustaining innovations to "break out" of a strategic group of similar firms in an industry. Consider these examples of sustaining innovations:

- the removal of high concentrations of sugar in breakfast cereals;
- the use of more powerful surfactants to boost the cleaning power of laundry detergents;
- the shift from reciprocating to rotary to scroll compressors in air conditioners;
- the growing ability of customers to track packages ordered from online retailers or websites;
- the use of new types of soy-based foams to insulate attics and walls in homes;
- the ability of eyewear lenses to change from clear to shaded when exposed to sunlight rather than artificial lighting.

These innovations represent important sources of value improvement to customers, but they typically do not change the rules of the game as to how organizations compete within their arenas in the industry. More important, it is quite easy for rivals to imitate and duplicate another firm's product modification or improvement.

On the other hand, firms can build a strong competitive advantage through determined and focused continuous improvement, especially when they face competitors experiencing organizational difficulties or bureaucratic procedures. These obstacles make it impossible to execute continuous improvements with speed and urgency. For example, the Toyota Motor Corporation has long pursued a policy of continuous product and process improvement to raise the value that customers receive when buying one of their vehicles. Toyota's commitment to excellence is well documented and can also be found across a wide spectrum of Japanese firms in different industries, all of whom practice "kaizen" (Japanese for "improvement") as part of their standard organizational processes.

During the last decade, we have witnessed the steady improvement in fuel efficiency and performance of gasoline-powered cars and trucks. Each automotive firm seeks to outdo its rivals through steady improvement of its product features, often by tinkering with existing engine and powertrain designs to boost efficiency and power. Vehicles run more efficiently and produce higher levels of performance, but their underlying core design remains wedded to a decades-long set of industry technical standards shaped around gasoline- or diesel-powered engines. These engines propel vehicles through controlled bursts of precisely calibrated mixtures of fuel and air in order to turn the engine. Specific examples of sustained innovations in the automotive industry include steady reductions in harshness, roughness, noise, and vibration when driving a vehicle; more precise fuel-injection systems, and new types of camshafts that replace pushrods in moving the engine's pistons. Toyota and Honda have been able to capture industry-leading positions through their own dedicated efforts, as well as from the inability of U.S. and European firms to execute fast continuous improvement on their own.

Seismic Upheavals—Changing Environmental Landscape

Industries are also subject to periods of "disruption," whereby unforeseen or new technologies, methods, or ways to serve customers completely redefine an industry's approach to creating value. As their name suggests, disruptive innovations "shake up" familiar ways of creating and delivering products to customers. A technological breakthrough or radically different way of serving the customer defines a disruptive innovation. The "disruption" can be so severe that an entire industry is transformed in a short time, much like a massive earthquake's impact on the surrounding landscape, which can divert rivers and cause avalanches. Disruptive innovations change the rules of the game for the entire industry; the industry's pre-existing methods and approaches, such as long-followed product designs, technical standards, or distribution channels, face the prospect of immediate obsolescence.

A monumental impact of a disruptive innovation is the extent to which an organization must learn an entirely new set of methods, skills and knowledge to come to grasp with the industry's redefined landscape. The more disruptive the innovation, the harder it is for senior managers to adjust to the new reality. Tried-and-tested product designs, manufacturing techniques, marketing methods, business processes, and ways to serve the customer can actually become barriers to learning and understanding the new reality.

In recent years, the number of industries impacted by a disruptive innovation seems to be growing. Consider the following "disruptions" that have unfolded over the past five years:

- new e-book readers transform how people read books and other so-called "print media";
- hand-held ultrasound devices allow physicians to capture body images without the need for massive hospital rooms and long waiting times for patients;
- advanced batteries and fuel cells supplant today's gasoline engines;
- nanotechnology-driven advances result in micro-machines that may be able to scrape plaque and fat deposits within human arteries;
- robotic surgical techniques dramatically slice healing and patient recuperative time;
- new "print" technologies enable semiconductor manufacturers to print circuits onto silicon wafers the way that people print photos at home with ink-jet or laser printers.

Let us now examine how these disruptions in progress have already begun to change the landscape for several companies. General Electric's HealthCare and Infrastructure businesses are at the cutting edge of research in both portable medical devices and in testing alternatives to jet turbine technology. GE is looking to its HealthCare unit to lead a number of similar innovations in digital patient records and digital imaging. Instead of the large pharmaceutical companies, it was the advanced laboratories of IBM that led the way in designing a nanotechnology-based drug that treats antibiotic-resistant staph infections. This is the same technology that IBM hopes to use in designing an entirely new line of semiconductors and advanced materials that bypass today's use of silicon. New models of DaVinci Robotics surgical systems (created by Intuitive Surgical) enable doctors to operate on patients with far less invasive procedures, resulting in much faster healing times. Using joysticks to control and manipulate small surgical tools, doctors can pinpoint exactly where and how much tissue to remove in the shortest time. 3-D "Print" technologies are still some way in the future, but they offer great promise to businesses in the electronics, flat-screen television and advanced materials fields to design miniature "fabs" (or factories) at ever smaller sizes and with much less environmental impact.

We have already witnessed the convulsions of industries already impacted by far-reaching disruptive technologies. Consider the following:

- the rise of retailing on the Internet over the past 15 years;
- the death of traditional film-based photography;
- the disappearance of pay phones and pagers as digital wireless phones became widespread;
- GPS-based systems have supplanted maps;
- digital MP3 music standards have rendered compact discs (CDs) a thing of the past;
- interactive set-top boxes that record movies and television shows (e.g., TiVo) have eliminated recordable DVDs.

From these examples, numerous firms across a host of industries struggled to grasp the reality and magnitude of a disruptive innovation. Eastman Kodak filed for bankruptcy protection in 2012 as the industry completed its near total transition to digital photography. Today, we may be witnessing another major tectonic shift in another industry: portable navigational aids. Garmin and TomTom are commonly found gadgets in cars to help drivers get to where they want to go. In the next few years, it is likely that both firms will feel the heat of new navigation technology built into GPS-enabled "smartphones."

The economic prospects of the Japanese consumer electronics giants Sony, Sharp and Panasonic have become much cloudier over the past few years as they face declining revenues and growing losses in their core consumer electronics businesses. All three firms have been slow to embrace the transition from analog to digital consumer gadgets, and ceded industry leadership to Apple and manufacturing strength to Samsung Electronics. Once the symbol of Japanese technological prowess, they are now playing catch-up to faster and larger competitors. The fate of these companies remains grim, even though they have practiced continuous improvement in their business operations for so long. Ironically, such a laser-like focus on improving existing products and processes blinded these firms to the larger changes reshaping the industry.

Disruptive innovations present another major challenge. Disruptive innovations often shake up an industry to such an extent that the business model of the impacted organizations is rendered completely useless. For example, the rise of Napster and the pervasiveness of MP3 music files in 1998 forced companies such as BMG, Polygram Records, EMI, Universal Music, Warner Music, and Sony Music to become web-based, digital distribution firms almost overnight. However, just several years previously, all of these firms had invested heavily in what they thought was the most modern manufacturing plant and equipment to stamp out compact discs in ultra-clean rooms that resemble microchip factories. Senior management across these organizations grappled without success for new ways to tackle such profit-draining issues as piracy, creating new distribution channels, learning about bandwidth issues, promoting new ways to listen to music, and retaining artists who looked at the Internet as a way to exit from their contracts with record label companies.

Fitting Together the Strategy Puzzle

A business strategy has many parts that must work together. One of the most powerful and useful frameworks developed in recent years to design business strategy was developed by Donald Hambrick and Jim

Fredrickson, who portray and elaborate the five major elements of strategy. Their work is captured in Figure 2.2 below.

Figure 2.2 describes any strategy as composed of five inter-related components that provide the basis for a mutually-reinforcing set of choices. These five components are:

1. arenas;
2. vehicles;
3. staging;
4. distinction;
5. economic logic.

Let us examine each of these and see how they represent vital guide-posts of any strategy. Effectively, a business chooses the customers it wishes to serve, designs the method to serve its customers, and selects the timing or sequence of moves as it enters the market. In turn, it must distinguish itself from its competitors. Doing these four things well enables it to be profitable.

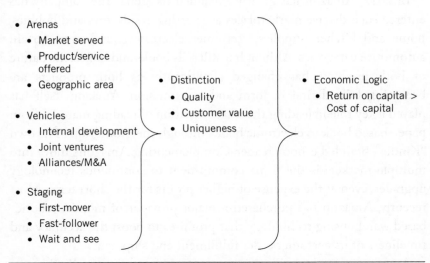

- Arenas
  - Market served
  - Product/service offered
  - Geographic area

- Vehicles
  - Internal development
  - Joint ventures
  - Alliances/M&A

- Staging
  - First-mover
  - Fast-follower
  - Wait and see

- Distinction
  - Quality
  - Customer value
  - Uniqueness

- Economic Logic
  - Return on capital > Cost of capital

Figure 2.2 Model of Business Strategy. Adapted from D.C. Hambrick & J. Fredrickson, "Do You Really Have a Strategy?," *Academy of Management Executive*, November 2001, Volume 15, pp. 48–59.[4]

Arenas

The word "arena" conjures up images of a gladiator in ancient Roman times dueling with other combatants or wild animals in an enclosed coliseum space. In those times, an arena was where combat occurred. Today, and in a business strategy context, an arena represents where the organization chooses to compete—in terms of choice of market segment, choice of product scope (wide or narrow), choice of technology(ies) used, and even the specific value-creating activities (design, manufacturing, order fulfillment, sales, service, etc.) that it selects.

Consider for example the arenas that Amazon.com chose to serve in 1996 and in 2012. In its earliest days, Amazon chose to sell music CDs and books. These were its arena. To enhance the prospects that new customers would flock to the company's website, Amazon chose to invest in state-of-the-art web design, supply chain systems, and order fulfillment software that would store a user's preferences, past orders, shipping addresses and billing information. Amazon's earliest customers tended to be those people who enjoyed surfing on the web and had access to personal computers at work or at home.

In 2012, Amazon has greatly expanded its arena. The company has entered such diverse marketplaces as sporting goods, toys and hobbies, home and kitchen supplies, consumer electronics, and even certain automotive categories. Although it still sells books and music, the nature of both products has changed significantly as both products are becoming fully digital in form and transmission. Amazon itself has played a key role in leading the transformation of reading material from paper-based book to electronic books through the promotion of its own "Kindle"-branded e-book reader. Complementing Amazon's move into multiple markets is the firm's commitment to continuous technology upgrades, even at the expense of higher profits for the short term. Most recently, Amazon has purchased a major provider of mobile, robotic-based warehousing technology that promises to boost the accuracy and timeliness of its customer order fulfillment and shipment.

An organization's choice of arenas arguably presents the single most pressing question in formulating strategy: it is analogous to the broader strategic question of "what business do we want to be in?" and compels senior management to think about the scope of what it wants to accomplish and the types of products, markets and technologies inherent in that choice.

Vehicles

Vehicles relate to the method by which a business enters an arena. How does a business actually enter a given market? How does a business acquire the technology used to serve its customers? Does it develop new products and services internally, or does it acquire an organization that already has them (make versus buy)? Conversely, does an organization partner with another business that already possesses the capability to help it accomplish its objectives? Or does it license its products or business formulas to others and let them enter new arenas, as ARM Holdings, Marriott International, Avis, Brinker International, and others have done over the years?

By its very nature, the choice of vehicle to enter an arena compels senior management to consider the tradeoffs that accompany such a choice. For example, a decision to develop products internally may yield significantly higher profit in the long run, but encumbers the firm with major fixed costs and a high degree of uncertainty in the short term. Conversely, an organization may choose to develop its own technological skill set to support its business (as Amazon has done), but often at great expense. However, partnering or allying with another firm to rely on its technology opens up a different set of tradeoffs—will the partner eventually become a competitor to our own business because it knows our strengths or vulnerabilities all too well? Some of the most common vehicles used to enter arenas include the following:

- internal development (also known as "organic growth")—a primary vehicle of Intel, Baxter International, and Sharp of Japan;
- strategic alliance (partnering with another firm to share costs and risks)—a vehicle used successfully by Nestlé, Corning, IBM, and Robex Resources, among others;
- acquisition (buying another firm that already has the requisite capabilities)—used by DuPont, Cisco Systems, the prescription drug delivery firm Express Scripts, and Aetna health insurance.

Staging

Staging refers to the sequencing of decisions and activities to support a strategy. Consider, for example, how many restaurant chains carefully invest in expanding their operations. Often, the company will operate their own company-owned stores to ensure that quality remains consistent across multiple outlets. Once the chain—such as Yum! Brands— has become sufficiently popular to justify further expansion, the firm will offer franchising opportunities that enable trained entrepreneurs to steadily bear the costs and efforts of further expansion at its Pizza Hut, KFC, and Taco Bell brands.

Let's briefly examine how Google has staged its entry into the mobile phone business. Best known for its powerful search engines and online advertising, Google invested profits from those businesses into developing a new type of digital phone software known as "Android." Designed to deliver a significant boost in cell phone versatility, Android has enabled Google to become a major player in the "smartphone" business. Users increasingly want phones that deliver more than simple voice communications, digital cameras, and music playing capabilities. The popularity of Android has propelled Google into a major competitor of Apple's line of iPhones and fostered the creation of literally thousands of additional applications ("apps") over the past few years. Google has used its software development expertise to expand beyond its original arenas (search engines and online advertising) to compete in a whole new arena (mobile phones). Google's staging involved two interconnected, sequential activities—first, to develop a major online presence where people can feel extremely comfortable while using the Internet; second, to transfer its software skills into a new operating system that takes advantage of how people have moved away from relying on personal computers as their primary digital appliance.

Carefully staging investments into a new market can yield significant returns for companies willing to experiment and to adjust their approaches as that market evolves. During the 1980s, Hyundai took small steps to create its own dealerships along the U.S. West Coast and major cities to serve its budding North American market. Since the United States represented an unknown, uncertain market for Hyundai at the time, it kept its initial investment low. Gradually, as consumers became more comfortable with purchasing a Hyundai-branded car, the company built ever-larger dealerships and was even wooed by large U.S. "mega-dealer" companies to become part of a larger collection of auto brands in an expanded auto mall concept. To reinforce its growing U.S. market share, in 2007 Hyundai built a $1.6 billion state-of-the-art assembly plant in Montgomery, Alabama, that now serves as a beachhead for further expansion into the North American market.

Distinction

Distinction is the heart of strategy. A business is only as profitable as it is distinctive. What attracts a customer to come to you and not someone else's business? If everyone were to produce a similar product with no distinguishing features, no one would profit. A business has no traction in the marketplace without something that distinguishes it from its competitors. The essence of distinction is that:

1. a business must do something better than its rivals;
2. it has to limit their ability to imitate or duplicate what it does well.

But those capabilities are based on systematic investments in skills and core competencies that enable the firm to separate itself from its rivals. Developing a base of distinctive, core competencies is one of the most important steps a firm can take to build long-term advantage. Core competencies themselves, however, do not equate to strategy.

How does an organization attain distinction? It is certainly no easy task, and requires direction, effort, and investment. Some general questions related to attaining distinction include the following:

•   Is the offering significantly better than that of the rival on some desired valuable attribute (e.g., quality, engineering, customer service, technical features, speed)?
•   Is the organization managing its internal operations in a way that is somehow faster, lower in cost, or more responsive to customers than its rivals?

- Does the organization offer something that is truly unique?
- Does the brand of the product or service make the customer feel comfortable or reassured in such a way that he/she keeps coming back?
- Does the customer's purchase reinforce the feeling that he/she feels benefited in some special way?
- Does the organization foster a unique or hard-to-imitate set of practices that promote faster innovation than its rivals?
- Is the organization's offering so specialized that there are no other providers?

These are just the most basic of questions: for any given product or service, the issues can certainly reach far deeper. Over the long term, an organization's source of distinction ultimately rests on developing an organization-specific set of capabilities that encourage its people to become creative in thinking about new and better ways to do things.

Economic Logic

Return on capital must exceed cost of capital. This is the iron law of economics that applies to each and every business. A firm must generate profits consistently over the long term to remain in business and compete effectively. Profits provide the fuel for future investment in the business.

In general, organizations make profits by either increasing their revenues (sales from customers) and/or reducing the cost of their operations (fixed and variable costs; direct and indirect—that accrue from running the business). Some organizations are able to thrive and develop enduring sources of competitive advantage by charging high prices for their products (e.g., jewelry firm Tiffany & Co., Swiss confectionery firm Lindt, Italian gun-maker Beretta, and the German automotive firms Daimler and BMW). On the other side of the equation, many firms generate strong profits through extremely lean and efficient operations (e.g., Wal-Mart Stores (retailing), McDonald's (fast food restaurants), Intel (semiconductors), and the Vanguard Group (mutual funds and financial services).

Creating Competitive Advantage

As can be seen from our discussion, translating a strategic vision into a powerful, concrete strategy demands that management think holistically and comprehensively about all of their key choices—arenas, vehicles, staging, sources of distinction, and economic logic. Each organization will need to do its own hard thinking. Although Hambrick and Fredrickson's framework and strategic guideposts can form an excellent baseline from which to think about these issues, strategic imperatives and capabilities that apply to one situation or firm will not necessarily apply to another; many variables and uncertainties impact the effectiveness of each organization's strategy. Let us now delve deeper into some of these imperatives.

Matching Environment with Strategic Choice

Business Environment

Crafting an effective strategy entails a comprehensive understanding of the environment that the business seeks to navigate in order to reach profitability. All firms face the pressure of meeting and serving their customers' needs. Over time, customers' expectations will change, sometimes in a very rapid way. In the short, medium or long term, businesses must understand, meet, and even exceed their customers' expectations to build competitive advantage. Likewise, gauging the nature of the environmental landscape is key to success. Industry change, whether measured and predictable or dramatic and game-changing, represents an unrelenting force that compels organizations to ante up their game and deliver ever higher levels of value to their customers. The nature of customer expectations, combined with the prospect for industry change in the competitive environment, provide the basis for understanding how organizations can adapt to a variety of challenges.

Strategic Choice

To provide managers with an integrated, comprehensive way of thinking about strategy, we construct a total, integrated picture. This "big picture view" melds together external industry dynamics with firm-centered strategic choices to examine how the five guideposts—arenas, vehicles, staging, distinction, and economic logic—will vary in line with the four basic strategies we introduced earlier—consolidator, pioneer, trendsetter, and reinventor.

Figure 2.3 presents the four strategies along with the capabilities businesses must build or hone to compete effectively given the

Consolidators		Reinventors	
Arenas:	Broad-line markets for standardized products	Arenas:	Mature markets impacted by disruption
Vehicles:	Long-term supplier relationships, selective mergers and acquisitions	Vehicles:	"Skunkworks," incubation of new businesses, strategic alliances with related firms; small bets
Staging:	Avoid being first-to-market with new products	Staging:	Sequencing is difficult due to cannibalization
Distinction:	Low-cost, standardized offerings	Distinction:	Resource allocation
Economic Logic:	Attain maximum scale to reduce costs; industry leader	Economic Logic:	Premium prices based on new products, or low cost to serve large markets
Trendsetters		**Pioneers**	
Arenas:	New market entry based on core product concept	Arenas:	New products, new core technologies
Vehicles:	Internal development of product concepts; related acquisitions	Vehicles:	Internal development and external licensing to larger firms
Staging:	Penetration and development of related products and neighboring geographic markets	Staging:	Quick speed of expansion into niche markets; first-to-market in R&D
Distinction:	Customer intimacy; set industry standards; branding	Distinction:	Key talent, fast innovation, patents
Economic Logic:	Superior pricing through customer loyalty, proprietary features or service	Economic Logic:	Generate high royalties from proprietary technology/patents, premium pricing from niche products

Customer Expectations: Known / Changing

Environmental Landscape: Stable — Changing

Figure 2.3 Framework for Strategic Choice.

landscape in which they find themselves. For organizations to "win," they need to build a portfolio of firm-specific capabilities to distinguish themselves from competitors. Figure 2.3 also demonstrates the roadmap that highlights the tradeoffs that accompany the choice of strategies.

MASTERING THE ESSENTIALS OF CRAFTING A STRATEGY

Mastering the essentials of crafting a strategy includes:

- choosing your arenas carefully;
- understanding the vehicles used to explore and enter your arena;
- creating a roadmap of sequential moves;
- building and exploiting sources of distinction;
- establishing key economic logic metrics to gauge performance.

Notes

1 Michael E. Porter, *Competitive Strategy*, Free Press, New York, 1980; M. E. Porter, *Competitive Advantage*, Free Press, New York, 1987.
2 The psychometric properties of the questionnaire instrument were determined by confirmatory factor analysis (CFA). These statistics include the following: n = 150; X2 = 172.10; degrees of freedom = 129; RMSEA = .058; CFI = .89.
3 Clayton M. Christensen, *The Innovator's Dilemma*, Harvard Business School Press, Boston, MA, 1997.
4 Donald C. Hambrick and James Fredrickson, "Do You Really Have a Strategy?," *Academy of Management Executive*, November 1, 2001, Volume 15, pp. 48–59.

3

STRATEGY IS NOT THE SAME FOR EACH ORGANIZATION

Effective execution depends on attaining co-alignment of four vital ingredients:

1. choice of strategy;
2. strategic disciplines;
3. organization design and culture;
4. leadership.

Senior managers need to ensure that these four ingredients mutually reinforce each other to build a competitive organization that delivers the desired results time and time again.

Building an Integrated Strategy

Managers must take an integrated approach to formulating and executing strategy. The strategic choices they make will directly impact arenas, choice of vehicles, speed of staging, areas of distinction, and economic logic. To be truly effective, a strategy should be thought out, formulated and "owned" by everyone who has to execute it. In most organizations, this means that strategy should be formulated jointly between senior management, key managers with profit and loss responsibility for a given business, and the direct reports who must take that strategy and implement it on a daily basis.

All too many organizations look at strategic planning as something done upstairs in the corporate suite, ignoring the fact that the people closest to customers, working in operations, and developing new technologies have the best vantage points with which to identify potential major threats and changes looming over the horizon, shifts in customer demand, and the potency of new, unforeseen competitors entering the same business space. These are the same people who can best gauge the risks involved, the ideas that are most likely to work, and the alternatives needed in case plans don't come to fruition. Ultimately, the leader of the business unit should own the strategy. Some key questions that senior people in any business should be able to answer include some of the following:

- Who is the competition?
- How well do we understand our customers, existing and future?
- What is the best way to grow the business?
- What are some looming threats?
- How will we compete? Will it be on cost, quality, innovation, or some combination?
- What are our short-term and long-term goals and objectives?
- Can we make money on an ongoing, sustainable basis, i.e., where is our profit sanctuary?

A useful, robust strategy is not merely crunching numbers or attending some worthless strategic planning meeting where one year's goals and objectives are merely a few per cent higher than a previous year's. Rather, a realistic and workable strategy demands a holistic view, insight, judgment, experience, and detail, all of which comes from the people situated close to the action and is owned by them. Understanding the issues critical for a business is not as good as having a strategic plan that lays out the specific actions and executable steps that people will take to achieve essential milestones.

Strategic Disciplines

A strategic discipline refers to the "guiding logic" that helps managers implement their strategy on a daily basis, as shown in Figure 3.1. Any business will utilize a number of strategic disciplines, but the priority of which discipline to emphasize depends on the strategic choice made by managers. A strategic discipline should also translate the business' strategy into specific, actionable results that directly emanate from employees' efforts to execute goals and objectives. The notion of a "discipline" rests on the link between higher-level strategy and a working premise that shapes the operating "context" of the business. These are some of the most salient strategic disciplines that we will discuss as they relate to any business:

- customer intimacy—service and execution that captures and retains customers;
- operational excellence—this deals with the entire range of issues related to converting inputs into outputs, procurement of inputs, information technology, logistics, and delivery;
- research and development—creating and commercializing the products that open up new business opportunities;
- resource allocation—managing the flow of funds and other resources among different business or product lines within the organization.

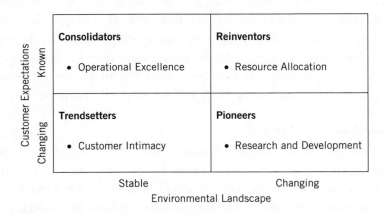

Figure 3.1 Mapping Strategic Disciplines with Strategy.

There is no doubt that every organization will need to develop some degree of competence across all four disciplines. However, a strategic discipline may become particularly relevant or assume a dominant priority in order to support the choices of a given strategy. Here are some examples of how various disciplines play a decisive role in supporting a larger organizational strategy.

Operational Excellence

A strategic discipline built on operational excellence is the foundation for McDonald's fast-food restaurant strategy. The absolute consistency and taste of French fries served at McDonald's restaurants, no matter where they are located, is the product of massive investment in developing a comprehensive supply chain that extends as far back as the farms that grow the potatoes. Working with giant potato supplier firms Simplot and McCain's, McDonald's jointly plans and assesses the best growing soil conditions that will yield the highest quality potatoes that meet its demanding standards. Both suppliers show McDonald's how the potatoes are grown and deliver them daily to processing plants in enormous quantities.

Likewise, an unwavering, laser-like focus on quality, repetition, and the highest product standards defines Intel's operations-driven discipline in managing its gargantuan, company-run chip plants. Every Intel semiconductor manufacturing plant is identical in terms of layout, equipment, format, and the internal flow of work. Using its long and deep experience in producing ever denser chips with cutting-edge technology, Intel ensures quality by conforming each fabrication plant to operate in precisely the same way according to exacting standards documented for each and every step of the production process.

Research and Development

Research and development (R&D) is the wellspring of bold new product ideas that can create entirely new industries if executed flawlessly and with perfect timing. R&D is the basis for many industries' existence, including software, semiconductors, pharmaceuticals, biotechnology, alternative energy, medical devices, engineered materials, and even advanced logistics and supply chain management systems. Although young organizations in science-intensive industries dedicate their entire existence to seeking product breakthroughs, large established companies continue to spend prodigiously on R&D to enhance and refine their products and processes.

In the pharmaceutical industry, for example, legendary firms such as Pfizer, Bristol-Myers Squibb, Novartis, Roche Holdings, and Merck continue to pour billions of dollars into exploring and experimenting with new molecules, methods, and scientific processes as they seek the next breakthrough cures for a host of human ailments. Smaller biotechnology companies—Amilyn Pharmaceuticals, Cephalon, and Human Genome Sciences, to name but a few—dedicate themselves to discovering and utilizing new molecular and genetic engineering techniques to identify, isolate, and contain the triggers of disease.

Many households have become enamored with their Roombas, a new kind of self-guided vacuum cleaner that cleans entire rooms by sensing where it needs to go and which corners and furniture to avoid. Created by a young firm known as iRobot, the Roomba has become a fast-growing, category-killer business in its own right. Increasing market demand has even attracted new entrants to the industry, including Neato Robotics, which plans to introduce a competing line of robotic vacuum cleaners in 2013.

Consider the enormous success that Nike has enjoyed as it conceives and delivers exciting sporting wear and gear to customers around the world. Although Nike is involved in producing its products across an extensive global network of factories, the company's strongest discipline relates to its ability to sense what trends and type of gear are likely to be hot in the sporting world. Nike's "sixth sense" in estimating what customers want—and how much they are willing to pay for it—is the foundation of its own fast innovation, R&D-driven discipline. Getting products to market is of course important, but for the most part Nike contracts the manufacturing of its products predominantly to Asian vendors who are responsible for timely delivery and compliance with fair standard work practices—an effort that requires continuous monitoring especially given the tragedy of 2011.

Customer Intimacy

Perhaps no organization can match Sewell Automotive's zeal and the pervasive ingrained belief that a business must earn each customer and do whatever it takes to retain him or her. Going "above and beyond" to serve customers is just the beginning of Sewell's approach to working with them: the company even expects to up the ante every year to serve its clients with new and bolder initiatives. To reach its ambitious customer service standards, Sewell sends managers to explore and watch how other leading-edge companies in other industries manage their businesses and deal with their own customer requirements.

While companies pursuing operational excellence concentrate on rendering their operations ever leaner and more efficient, those pursuing a discipline of customer intimacy continually tailor, refine, and shape products and services to their customers' requirements. These changes can be expensive, but companies with this focus are willing to spend to build enduring customer loyalty, and indeed often measure a customer's lifetime value to the organization, rather than a single, one-off transaction. Along with Sewell, firms such as Nordstrom, Dyson, The Home Depot, Wegmans, L. L. Bean, and The Container Store seek to build a very long-term relationship with their customers.

Sewell Automotive knows that not all customers demand the same level of service or will generate the same revenues. Carl Sewell, the CEO, knows that profitability depends upon refining a system that distinguishes rapidly and accurately between those customers' desired degrees of service, and the patronage they are likely to generate. For example, buyers of Cadillac and Lexus products are likely to demand more attention to service than those purchasing GMC vehicles.

Similarly, The Home Depot associates are instructed to spend whatever time is needed with customers to solve their home improvement needs. They're not just being nice; executing customer intimacy as a discipline requires that they pay close attention to what their customers want and their service requirements. When Bob Nardelli tried to impose an "operations excellence" discipline at the expense of customer intimacy, he was ultimately ousted as CEO. Although The Home Depot's meteoric growth over the 1980s and 1990s required some streamlining to control costs, Nardelli's excessive focus on cost drove away customers and the vital store associates who possessed the knowledge and skills that could help them. In fact, for much of the past decade, The Home Depot's stock performance under Nardelli (stagnant) contrasted sharply with that of arch-rival Lowe's (steadily rising).

Resource Allocation

Effective management and utilization of organizational resources is a vital skill that sustains business growth momentum. Resource allocation capabilities are especially relevant to organizations facing the need to reorient and shift their strategies in the wake of major environmental change, or the sudden rise of new opportunities and threats to their business models.

For example, major U.S. defense contractors, such as Raytheon, Lockheed-Martin, Boeing, and Northrop-Grumman, now confront the prospect of significantly reduced defense spending in the wake of massive budgetary and debt-reduction pressures by the United States Congress. These organizations are caught in the vise between the need to look for ways of reducing costs on existing defense programs, while simultaneously exploring and testing advanced new technologies that could dramatically change tomorrow's battlefield. Allocating a shrinking "pie" of federal dollars to the most important projects represents a constant test of the resource allocation skills for all of these firms.

In subsequent chapters, we demonstrate how the importance and priority of strategic disciplines can vary across the strategies chosen by senior management to navigate the economic landscape facing them.

Organization Design

Many managers will probably remember from their business school classes the term "organization design." This broad phrase is a catchall that encompasses all of the components of organizational structure, reward systems, career development paths, and other dimensions. Businesses cannot execute their chosen strategy without ensuring that their organization design supports it. The dimensions that we will cover in this book include:

- organizational structure;
- performance evaluation/reward systems (soliciting and changing desired behaviors);
- culture (beliefs, norms, and what is appreciated and valued).

We will examine each of these dimensions as they relate to developing the necessary skill sets, behaviors, and mindsets that represent the day-to-day workings of an organization.

Although it is an arduous and time-consuming process, building a structure that reflects an organization's strategy and culture has proven worthwhile time and time again. Creating a change to facilitate this alignment is often difficult, and this is especially true for companies that have been around for a long period of time. Three or four decades are plenty of time for a company to become a dinosaur, unable to adapt to the demands of its new environment. 40 years of senior managers all singing the same hymns builds enormous resistance to structural change when new conditions arise that challenge traditional ways of doing business. As a result, fewer than 70 companies that made the Fortune 500 list in 1955 are still in business today.

In the 1990s, Caterpillar embarked on a program to identify obstacles to reaching its revenue and cost goals. This led to the identification of nine common values (trust, teamwork, mutual respect, empowerment, risk taking, sense of urgency, continuous improvement, commitment and customer satisfaction) that would drive the day-to-day behaviors of all employees. Implementing the program was not easy. When one realizes that 90 per cent of patients who have had coronary bypasses eventually end up returning to their former unhealthy lifestyles, why should we expect any company to behave any differently? A company's structure is an analog or reflection of its leadership's behavior, much like a marionette's behavior is an analog of the puppeteer's hand motions. Leaders try to preserve their worldview because it gives them confidence in their judgments, beliefs and actions. This is why protection of a company's structure often overrides a pragmatic need to change. Union employees were not receptive to changes and some upper levels of management whose management style was incompatible with these common values were outplaced. Employees gradually came to embrace the program, however, as they realized that the traditional hierarchical structure would no longer permit Caterpillar to remain competitive, especially in the wake of intensifying competition from a revitalized Komatsu of Japan and even newer, more agile competitors based in emerging markets such as China. For the first time, employees and management communicated and silos were broken down. To ensure lasting changes, the company adopted a "Cultural Assessment Program" that allows the company to identify changes that can lead to improvements and cost reductions. It has been deployed worldwide. Division managers are required to inform all divisional employees of the assessment results and the resulting action plans. As a result, unfavorable information is conveyed to executive management as soon as it is identified, instead of being concealed. This allows the company to act on bad news constructively and in a timely manner.

Similarly, the design firm IDEO operates with a flat structure. There are few levels between frontline employees and senior managers. Since the founders had previously worked in hierarchically driven organizations, they were determined to do things differently. Employees are encouraged and rewarded to come up with ideas without fear of expressing their thoughts openly.

Employees at Southwest Airlines are "cross-trained" so that they can perform multiple tasks and vary their job assignments. The very nature of this cross-functional training among employees, and the expectation of shared work experiences, makes for a highly potent competitor in the brutal airline business. Cross-training enables Southwest to eliminate the cumbersome job descriptions and lengthy communication procedures that add to expenses and raises the risks of delays. Southwest still outpaces all of the major U.S. carriers in terms of how quickly it can turn round planes landing and taking off from U.S. airports.

The Leadership Imperative

There is an ancient Chinese saying, likely of Taoist origin, that goes something like this: Leaders who do not encourage their people to become leaders are not really leaders. As convoluted as this may sound, there is a lot of truth in this statement. The ultimate job of any leader is to develop his/her people. Working through people to execute desired strategies, goals, and objectives is the essence of leadership.

Translating a vision into a coherent, integrated strategy that is reinforced with well developed strategic disciplines and supported by a vibrant organization design is the big picture job of leadership. Leaders bring all organizational assets into play and provide the direction that unifies everyone's efforts. To sustain competitive advantage:

- leaders convert organizational beliefs into desired behaviors;
- leaders create the expectations and performance milestones to which their people aspire and reach;
- leaders' behaviors directly shape the culture of a company. When leaders change their behaviors, they also change organizational cultures;
- leadership is also about growing their people's potential, not merely ensuring that the right person fits the right job today.

Ultimately, leaders have one overriding task: designing a system that stretches people's capabilities and develops them for the right positions in the future. If these ideas seem so obvious, then why do so many organizations seem incapable of putting these leadership concepts into practice?

MASTERING THE ESSENTIALS OF EXECUTING A STRATEGY

Mastering the essentials of executing strategy involves:

- understanding strategic disciplines;
- matching strategic disciplines with the appropriate strategy;
- designing a structure to support the strategy;
- selecting the right leaders to support the strategy.

4

PIONEERS

Pioneers are the lifeblood of every industry in every economy. No industry ever begins without the kind of bold risk-taking that all too often fails, unnoticed. From their inception, economies around the world have depended on pioneers to create new products and technological breakthroughs that have seeded entirely new ways of doing things. From an earlier time, such illustrious pioneering names as John Deere, General Electric, Westinghouse Electric, Otis Elevator, Sikorsky Helicopter, Eastman Kodak, Ampex, and FMC were synonymous with the industry they created in the United States. As these firms grew, they transformed the lives of their customers, provided millions of jobs to employees, and created hundreds of billions of dollars of wealth to their shareholders.

Today, pioneering firms are just as important, if not more so, as they create leading-edge products and solutions to many of the twenty-first century's most intractable problems. Point to any human need and most likely you will find a person or a team of people scrambling for a solution. In science-driven fields, such as biotechnology, alternative energy, nanotechnology, software, telecommunications, and computers, thousands of entrepreneurs, scientists, and thinkers of all stripes are devoting their entire lives to search for a better future for humankind. In other industries, ranging from restaurants, to consumer products, home health care, cleaning supplies, and education, energetic entrepreneurs from all backgrounds and life stories relentlessly experiment with new ideas and bold approaches to deliver better value to customers. Yet, most of us rapidly forget the inventions and breakthroughs of pioneers that transform our lives.

In today's complex economy, the role of pioneers cannot be understated. In each and every industry, there are bold risk-takers who have changed the way that customers eat, work, play, live, stay healthy, and attain personal growth and satisfaction. Let us take a look at some of the pioneering companies that are creating value in completely new and unexpected ways. And they are not high-tech outfits either! Figure 4.1 illustrates the key components that make up the foundation of a Pioneer.

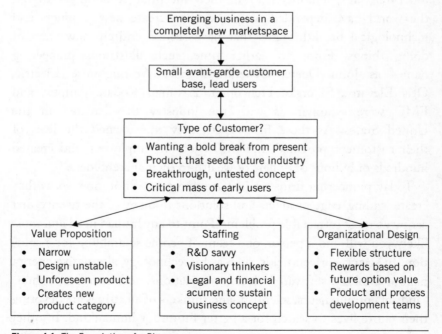

Figure 4.1 The Foundation of a Pioneer.

From Chips to Food to Apps

The food industry is replete with pioneers who have created new types of foods, recipes, and formats to fulfill the world's growing palate. Think about Ray Kroc of McDonald's and you already have a legendary classic American business success story that dates from the mid-1950s. Or in the grocery store, look no further than the frozen food aisle. Clarence Birdseye transformed the way the world eats through his pioneering idea of freezing food to preserve its freshness, and now almost every supermarket stocks Birdseye products. Believing in practical solutions and hard work, Birdseye noticed that fishermen in Canada immediately put their catch on ice in order to prevent spoilage. Using mass-production industrial processes reminiscent of Henry Ford and Andrew Carnegie, Birdseye developed a fast-freezing technology that worked for all types of meats and vegetables. This meant food no longer needed to be stored in brine or through other foul-smelling methods. There was no food with which Birdseye would not experiment. Whether he was freezing fish, meat, vegetables, or bread, Birdseye's main aim was to get the product from producer to wholesaler to retailer in the most efficient, sanitary, and convenient packaged form. In the process of experimenting and learning, Birdseye earned patents for his fast-freezing processes and the machines that would ultimately become ubiquitous at every convenience store and supermarket worldwide. Birdseye would later sell his company for $23 million to a firm that would become known as General Foods.[1] Despite being synonymous with frozen food, Birdseye would continue researching and inventing new ways to preserve food: from freeze-dried techniques to hydroponic farming, he sincerely believed that through technology, man would eventually conquer hunger worldwide.

Have you ever enjoyed a delightful snack chip made from a bagel? If you did, chances are you ate a light and crunchy chip conceived by a restaurateur who came up with the idea of mincing bagels into thin slices and then baking them into small, round chips. How did this idea come about? According to legendary accounts, a Boston-based caterer, known as Stacy, owned a sandwich shop whose popularity compelled her customers to wait in line for service, sometimes for too long. To ensure her customers would not leave, she began to slice her bagels, bake them, and offer them as free samples to assuage the hungry horde. Eventually the bagel chips became so popular that they started to outsell her sandwiches. Soon after, this small outfit was purchased by no other than the huge snack food giant, Frito-Lay, a unit of PepsiCo.

Ironically, the manufacture and distribution of chips laid the foundation for Frito-Lay itself. In 1932, C. Doolin enjoyed a meal at a San Antonio restaurant and purchased a bag of corn chips. Doolin soon learned that the manufacturer of the corn chips was willing to sell his business. He acquired it and began to sell Fritos Corn Chips from his Model T Ford. Coincidentally that same year, Herman W. Lay started selling potato chips in Nashville as a distributor for a small manufacturer. Lay eventually purchased the company, and the Lay's Potato Chip Company rapidly became one of the biggest snack food companies in the Southeast. Later in 1961, the two companies would merge to become Frito-Lay, Inc.[2]

Today, consider the enormous popularity of the Rachel Ray show in the United States. Her cookbooks, television shows, recipes, and cuisine ideas began with her early efforts to promote the novel concept of "Thirty Minute Meals" during the 1990s when she worked at a series of family restaurants, New York department stores, and gourmet shops. She noticed that many customers of all income levels did not enjoy cooking for themselves. Her "Thirty Minute Meals" concept became popular enough that a local New York television station asked her to appear occasionally to demonstrate some of her fun and easy-to-make recipes to viewers. Her popularity grew when she also wrote her first book, leading to a highly coveted slot on the Food Network in 2001. In 2005, the famous talk show host Oprah Winfrey re-discovered Rachel Ray and asked her to appear periodically on her afternoon TV show. Ultimately, this series of viewings led Oprah Winfrey and King World Productions the following year to create the daytime program, "The Rachel Ray Show." Many people credit the now-famous recipe creator for rekindling an interest in home cooking by emphasizing the joy of making meals from scratch without adhering to excessively rigid standards of measuring and timing while preparing food.

If Rachel Ray is increasingly associated with the ease and enjoyment of food preparation, then Hot Pockets may be synonymous with the creation of fast, convenient, microwavable sandwiches. What is the relevance of Hot Pockets to the U.S. food scene? Created during the 1980s by a company previously known as Chef America, Inc., Hot Pockets created an entirely new food category—the microwavable frozen sandwich with a hot inside and a tasty crunch on the outside. Based on a patented, proprietary special dough and filling combination, Chef America combined the best features of refrigerated storage, convenience, and microwave cooking to popularize a completely new way of eating. Hot Pocket sandwiches come packed with a special "sleeve" that channels the microwave oven's heat to the sandwich dough, thereby creating a distinctively light and crispy, crunchy texture. Building on the concept's speed and ease, Chef America then introduced the Lean Pockets brand in 1987 for health-conscious customers. In 2002, Chef America created a whole new line of Hot Pocket breakfast sandwiches that incorporated eggs and cheese into a tasty morning treat. Later that year, Swiss food giant Nestlé purchased Chef America from the controlling Merage family for $2.6 billion. With its global heft, Nestlé now sells the Hot Pockets and Lean Pockets line of sandwiches throughout the world, including Mexico, France, Germany, and the United Kingdom under a local brand name.[3]

Have you wanted to combine a top-of-the-line steakhouse dining experience with the benefits of all-you-can-eat? This novel, bold concept is the brainchild of Jair and Arri Coser and Jorge and Alexio Ongarotto. Together they started a restaurant known as "Fogo de Chao Churrascaria" in their hometown of Porto Alegre, Brazil in 1981. The four of them grew up on family farms and met while working as busboys at restaurants in Rio de Janiero. Determined not to return to the brutal, hot work of their childhoods, the partners opened up their first Fogo in an old, shed-like café that had a strongly rustic ambience. Today, patrons at Fogo de Chao in Brazilian cities, as well as numerous U.S. locations, can enjoy endless slivers of various meats paraded to their tables sliced by trained gauchos wielding samurai-like knives, along with enormous, seemingly endless salad bars featuring some exotic vegetables and fruits.

In 2011, the privately held company was believed to have brought in over $200 million in revenues. A Brazilian private equity firm owns about 35 per cent of the company, with the four partners owning the remainder. Fogo de Chao believes in funding new restaurants through existing cash flow. This growth policy means that it never opens more than one restaurant in any given metropolitan area. In 2012, the company opened several new locations, including one in Rio de Janiero, Brazil, as well as sites in Las Vegas and Orlando in the U.S. The company notes that it is not unusual to serve a thousand people on a Saturday night, often at $65 per person on average. Despite his phenomenal success, Jair Coser remains modest and believes in rewarding top performers. Top gauchos in Fogo restaurants make up to $100,000 per year, while general managers can make up to $400,000. He believes in his vision of blending the best of Brazilian gaucho-style cooking and service with American tastes.[4]

In the digital information age, we all take for granted that we use the personal computer (PC) for our homes, offices, businesses, or industrial applications. When people think about PCs, they often associate it with writing papers, communicating with people through e-mail, or perhaps gaming. Yet, how many people remember the name Jack Tramiel, who died in April 2012? Unlike Steve Jobs' original Apple Computer, or Bill Gates' original Microsoft PC software, Jack Tramiel pioneered one of the first home PCs, known as the "Commodore 64." A visionary entrepreneur who survived the Holocaust, Tramiel founded Commodore after having started his life in America as a typewriter repairman working for the U.S. Army. Commodore began its business importing typewriter and typewriter parts, but soon expanded into electronics after Tramiel witnessed the fast rise of Japanese calculators and other simple devices. Commodore introduced its first PC in 1977, the same year that Apple introduced its own Apple II. When the Commodore 64 appeared in 1982, it would soon become one of the best selling home-based personal computers of all time. In 1984, Tramiel left the company he founded and subsequently purchased Atari, a troubled company seeking to enter the electronic video game market. One of Tramiel's greatest personal accomplishments was the creation of more millionaires at Commodore than at any other firm.[5] Tramiel's legendary accomplishments go far beyond that of creating a simple electronic device—his vision of home-based computing powered the creation of many new supporting industries in Silicon Valley in their own right.

Yet, exploiting the full potential of the PC to communicate and perform novel tasks would not be possible without the brilliant work of Marc Andreessen. He invented the browser at age 22 while an undergraduate student working at the supercomputer center at the University of Illinois. The browser, known initially as Mosaic, later found its way to Silicon Valley, where Andreessen co-founded Netscape, one of the most legendary Internet-based start-ups of all time. By August 1995, the company had gone public at a then-meteoric $2.9 billion IPO. Andreessen's graphic browser laid the foundation for popularizing the Internet and bringing it into tens of millions of homes and offices. Although Netscape ultimately lost the "browser wars" with Microsoft's Internet Explorer, Andreessen's vision of launching an endless number of Internet-focused "apps" from PCs and other hardware devices has stood the test of time. Currently, Andreessen is pushing forth his vision where every business will begin to run their entire operations through a concept known as "cloud computing," where extremely inexpensive servers and virtual software will transform every business into a web business. With "cloud computing," companies and people will no longer have to download the latest "app" or data on their personal devices—a visit to each website will represent an opportunity to interact with the latest update or version of any feature needed.[6]

Strategic Issues for Pioneers

As we can see from these examples, Pioneers from all industries are risk-takers that thrive in highly uncertain, dynamic environments. Without exception, Pioneers must persevere and fight to stay alive, especially when the barriers to entry and exit are often quite low. One of the most daunting uncertainties confronting Pioneers is how best do they gauge their customers' expectations and then develop a method to serve them. By their very nature, Pioneers identify some type of unmet need and strive to find some way of fulfilling it. Even when an industry is dominated by pre-existing large firms, successful Pioneers often re-define the competitive marketplace and ultimately create an entirely new product category (e.g., online brokerage services) or an industry (e.g., frozen food, PCs).

At the heart of Pioneers' competitive advantage is the notion of a *first-mover advantage*,[7] that occurs when a firm has the opportunity to introduce a new product in an existing market, to create a new market, or to create value in a new way for its customers. Often, the first-mover advantage relies on a lead in some key technology, way of innovating, or business process that other firms will find difficult to imitate, at least initially. In practice, this means that Pioneers rely heavily on developing and protecting their knowledge-based assets, including intellectual property (e.g., patents, copyrights, trademarks) or proprietary methods (e.g., production methods, formulas, techniques), or even the firm's brands and other reputation sources. Table 4.1 highlights the major strategic issues confronting Pioneers.

To translate a first-mover advantage into a strong competitive position, Pioneers need to be able to reach, capture, and retain customers quickly. A powerful value proposition is essential to doing this. For example, a Pioneer may make it much easier for customers to purchase products and services as airline start-ups People Express and Virgin Atlantic did in the 1980s and 1990s respectively. By redefining the value chain in a way that bypassed established distribution channels, both airline start-ups caught legions of enthusiastic customers who flocked to their packed jets. Likewise, Dell Computer created a novel (at the time) way of selling computers to customers—through the telephone and later the Internet. Customers could order custom-made Dell PCs

---

Table 4.1 Key Strategic Issues for Pioneers

- Creating a compelling vision
- Investigating R&D
- Securing lines of credit/capital
- Avoiding long-term supplier arrangements

and have them delivered straight to their home or office. In other cases, Pioneers can also capture customers by setting a standard of service that earns customers' ongoing brand loyalty. For example, the tremendous success that Sony enjoyed over three decades emanated from the Japanese firm's commitment to designing and building the very best quality consumer electronics products available. Sony's breakthrough designs for the Walkman (1970s), the compact disc (in conjunction with Philips NV in 1982), the Mini-Disc (early 1990s) and the PlayStation series of video-game consoles over the last ten years is testament to the firm's fast-design capabilities that win and retain successive generations of customers.

Pioneers tend to be small firms and often have founders with great vision and passion for doing something that most people think impossible—or even insane. Sometimes this vision extends to break-through technologies (e.g., web browsers or disease cures); other times, these visions relate to a better way of doing things (e.g., Richard Branson's forays into the music, retailing, and airline businesses); or a superior way of delivering a customer experience (e.g., Jani-King in the office cleaning business); or certainly a way of thinking about the customer when designing products (e.g., Sony under late CEO Akio Morita). Pioneers rely on agility, enormous sweat equity, and speed of product development to create bold new product ideas that set or re-define the standards of customer expectations.

Pioneers cannot count on the presence of a large customer base to amortize their investment costs. Customers who buy Pioneers' products tend to be enthusiasts who want the "new toy," or disgruntled customers turned off by the stale offerings of existing firms. For example, a young Richard Branson, a publisher of a student-oriented newspaper, first got into the music retailing business when he realized that college students received terrible treatment at the established music stores surrounding universities and schools. Branson saw an opportunity to transform the way students purchased music by starting a mail-order retailing format. By advertising the notion of buying music without standing in line at stuffy, older retail establishments in his student newspaper, Branson tapped into a hidden, unmet need. Students would pre-pay for the music records they wanted to hear, and Branson's workforce of young college students would mail it to them after ordering large quantities of records from other distant, lower-priced retailers. Ultimately, this business became known as Virgin Music.[8]

Arenas

It is the novelty of the concept that attracts customers to Pioneers. Unlike more established firms, they often confine their initial *arenas* to specialized niches that find a more amenable customer base for breakthrough products, technologies, or new ways of doing business. Pioneers and their founding leaders must be intimately familiar with the specific needs or technologies that match what they believe will be the exact needs of a particular set of customers. Even though the specific customer requirements are often shrouded in uncertainty, a Pioneer's leader possesses an overriding vision to make the dream a reality. Too broad a range of product offerings works against the sharp, almost maniacal focus that is necessary for Pioneers to survive.

If a Pioneer develops an end product, it probably meets the needs of a specialized niche initially, rather than a mass market. In the January 1975 issue of *Popular Electronics*, the cover story was about a machine called the "Altair 8800." It cost $397. It was a do-it-yourself contraption that you could assemble at home. The machine was the first PC. IBM and other mainframe computer companies ignored this electronic breakthrough because it was too small and inexpensive to be relevant to their product market space. Altair eventually went bankrupt because none of the large mainframe companies was willing to invest money in the project. On the other hand, Commodore introduced its version of the PC in 1977, just as Apple and TRS did. These early machines performed rudimentary computing tasks but became the basis for what would be gargantuan industries just a few years later.

In many instances, Pioneers seek to aggressively develop and license their technologies to other firms who may be better positioned to assume the risks of fully fledged market development. It is often the case that when Pioneers attempt to license their technologies or idea to established firms, they meet a tremendous amount of skepticism. When established companies examine and review a Pioneer's concept or proto-type, they often think this: if there was a better way of designing a product or service, then somebody here must have already considered it and discarded the idea. For example, Chicopee Mills first introduced the disposable diaper in 1932. By 1956, only 1 per cent of consumers were buying them. The main reason was cost, around $0.09 per diaper. Later, in 1962, Procter & Gamble acquired the company. Through their efficient marketing and manufacturing capabilities, P&G drastically reduced the price to less than $0.03 per diaper. Today, Pampers commands 15 per cent market share of this $22 billion market.

Consider the future growth of electric automobiles. Perhaps the one name most associated with this rapidly growing niche is Tesla Motors. Lead investor Elon Musk, who scored huge profits after founding and selling PayPal to eBay in 2002, believed that Tesla can transform the way the auto industry builds cars. Since electric vehicles are inherently more efficient and environmentally friendly than combustion engines, they would be a real boon to reducing energy consumption. Started in 2004 with funding coming from Silicon Valley investors, Tesla Motors' initial business plan had ambitious goals, the first being to build a really cool, high-end and ultra-performance sports car to prove the viability of the electric car concept. Ultimately, Tesla hoped to mass-produce more affordable models for the general public in its quest to rid the world of carbon-based emissions from conventional fossil fuels. Yet, Tesla's first foray with the electric car—the $109,000 Tesla Roadster—encountered innumerable problems when introduced in 2007. It was about to go into production when internal cost audits showed that it took another $30,000 dollars than previously thought to actually build the vehicle, meaning that Tesla was losing enormous amounts of money on each car. Still, Tesla's engineers focused on the core components that drove the electric car: the lithium-ion battery pack and a novel design for the car's electric motor. The battery pack and the electric motor defined the initial arena around which Tesla focused its efforts.

Tesla's big break came when executives from Daimler-Benz of Germany, the producer of the Mercedes line of cars, announced a visit to Tesla's facilities after they had initially expressed skepticism about

Musk's vision. Jumping on the opportunity, Musk and his engineers began retrofitting a Daimler Smart car with a Tesla battery pack and motor in five weeks. When Daimler executives first saw the Smart car, they did not discern any differences. But when they drove it, they realized it was much more powerful and agile than the conventional model that Daimler produced. Daimler then proposed a deal with Tesla to begin designing and co-producing battery packs for electric Smart cars for sale in Europe. To boot, Daimler also contributed $50 million for an equity stake in the company.

Tesla's importance and influence in the broader automotive industry is impossible to underestimate. Another Tesla co-founder started a competing electric vehicle company in 2005. Other Tesla engineers now lead the battery production efforts at a separate company, while another heads up the entire battery operation at Volkswagen. Toyota Motor of Japan now works with Tesla to produce battery-powered RAV4's in the United States—ironically at a plant that Tesla bought from Toyota for $42 million at the depth of the 2008 recession.[9] Table 4.2 captures the arena-related issues for Pioneers.

Vehicles

Pioneers need to be able to reach their customers. To get its ideas or product concept to market, many Pioneers rely on a new technology or distribution channel. In other instances, Pioneers license their product ideas, proprietary processes, brand names, or other knowledge-based assets to larger, established firms. Established firms often have the strategic capabilities (e.g., extensive distribution channels, economies of scale in production and operations) that Pioneers lack.

Table 4.2 Key Arena Issues for Pioneers
• Create market demand
• Shape customer expectations
• Avoid direct competition with established firms
• Do not overcommit resources

Consider the rise of the Dollar Shave Club. A start-up firm with only six employees, the Dollar Shave Club has already raised over $1 million in seed funding from wealthy "angel investors" and venture capitalists. The Dollar Shave Club tapped into an unmet need among men. Most men like to keep down the cost of replacing their blades after each shave; some individuals will go as far as to wash their blades in a dishwasher or even clean them with a toothbrush in order to avoid purchasing expensive replacement blades. The Dollar Shave Club combines a subscription-based sales model that connects online ordering with home delivery of a low-cost supply of blades. There are three different subscription plans for which men can sign up. For example, a subscriber can pay $3 a month for a two-blade razor plan, whereby the customer receives a razor and a supply of blades for that razor every month. For men who use a four-blade razor, the price is adjusted upwards accordingly.

The primary vehicle for the Dollar Shave Club is the use of new technologies, such as YouTube videos that demonstrate how the Club works, often through humor generated by comedians who poke fun at the start-up. With no marketing budget, the Dollar Shave Club can win over parades of customers through a digital following on such online forums as Twitter and Facebook. In many ways, the Dollar Shave Club has already stirred up so much interest that more established firms— Procter & Gamble's Gillette and Energizer Holdings, for example— are beginning to consider changes to the way they sell their razors and blades.[10]

The Dollar Shave Club's use of technology to circumvent existing distribution channels and selling approaches reflects the growing expectation by customers that products and services should be easier to buy over time. Over the past decade companies such as Amazon, Apple, Overstock, and Netflix have paved the way for "conditioned" customers to expect growing convenience in their routine purchases. Other start-up firms that have tapped into this unmet need in other product universes include Zappos.com for shoes.

To prevent competitor imitation, Pioneers need to keep their idea chests full with new product designs and concepts. The great threat facing Dollar Shave Club, Zappos.com, and other similar start-ups is that established businesses in their respective markets recognize the potential threats posed by these Pioneers. When Pioneers offer a compelling value proposition by using a new technology or distribution method, the established firm must be quick to react to the challenge. Pioneers can wreak great havoc on an established business' pricing and distribution if customers switch to the start-up. More important, these types of customers are often highly fluent and vocal in their use of social media (Facebook and Twitter) to communicate their likes and dislikes. As mindshare becomes ever more dependent on customer responses and feelings expressed in constantly updated social media forums, this presents a great opportunity for Pioneers to respond and to adjust quickly to customers' needs. The leanness and flexibility of Pioneers' operations makes them better able to respond than established businesses.

In the future, it is likely that social media forums will become very important vehicles for many entrepreneurs seeking to reach masses of customers as quickly as possible. For example, Facebook, itself a Pioneer in the explosive world of social networking, has already captured some 900 million users (at the time of writing). The widespread availability of smartphones, combined with the ubiquity of Facebook and Twitter, promise to open new opportunities for firms of all types to learn about their customers' experiences. Pioneers, in particular, must be able to surf the waves of social media to quickly adjust to what their customers want, since they need to earn customer loyalty fast. Related to the exponential growth of social media is the notion of "crowdsourcing," whereby lead customers begin to actively work with businesses to co-design and co-develop future offerings. Crowdsourcing can empower Pioneers to accelerate their product development and refinement time to better meet fast-changing customer needs. However, crowd-sourcing may also represent a double-edged sword to the extent that larger, better-funded established businesses line up to learn how to take advantage of this trend too.

The potency of social networking and web-driven communities has already created the ferment for an entirely new forum known as "social gaming." This trend has already powered a come-from-nowhere start-up called Zynga, which currently runs 18 highly addictive online gaming communities. Amazingly, Zynga has captured almost 300 million people a month to play its virtual games, gaining it some $1.1 billion in revenues at the end of 2012. It now owns the most popular online games (e.g., *CityVille, Zynga Pokes, FarmVille*) ever created and it has a fast-growing app on Facebook.[11] According to Mike Kidd, Project Manager for Zynga's Dallas operation, the company is also using browser-based games that work both on stand-alone and mobile platforms, such as Apple iOS and Google Android, and as application widgets on social networking websites including Facebook, Zynga.com, Google, and Tencent. During Zynga's five-year contract with Facebook, all those games that use the social networking site's integration must remain exclusive to it. This accounts for 12 per cent of Facebook's revenue. According to this agreement, Zynga is not allowed to release new games to other social networks and must notify Facebook of any new games at least one week prior to their release. Zynga is trying to create its own platform in which users can play company games in its attempt to break away from its dependence on Facebook. Table 4.3 outlines the vehicles most often used by Pioneers.

Staging

Pioneers must be extremely careful in how they stage their activities, particularly as resources are tight. They must maintain a laser-like focus on a narrowly defined arena. For Pioneers, how activities are sequenced (or staged) depends on cash inflow and the customers' receptivity to the initial product. In the late 1990s, for example, Rachel Ray's success with offering ideas for "Thirty Minute Meals" as an occasional guest on local

---

Table 4.3 Key Vehicle Issues for Pioneers

- Promote new R&D approaches
- Create innovative distribution channels/methods
- Form joint ventures and other alliance arrangements

television shows earned her growing popularity to the point where her recipe and cookbooks became major successes.

When James Dyson first invented his air cyclone-based design vacuum cleaner in the early 1980s, he licensed the idea to a Japanese appliance company who manufactured it in a pink color-way and sold it under the G-Force name in Japan. The machine was an immediate hit as customers viewed it as a fashion statement, rather than a cleaning device. Sales from the G-Force machines helped fund Dyson's investment in manufacturing and equipment, enabling him to build his own machines in Britain. Dyson felt he needed to build the machine on his own because some of his earlier licensing deals with U.S. and European manufacturers got him nowhere.[12]

In the case of Zynga, Mark Pincus founded the firm in April 2007 in San Francisco. Its first game, *Texas Hold'Em Poker*, was released on Facebook in July 2007. With some $10 million in venture capital, Zynga was able to rapidly develop new games and open new offices. It quickly became Facebook's Number One app. Within two years—and after acquiring a game studio in Baltimore in 2009—it launched *FarmVille*. Two months later, it was the first game on Facebook to reach ten million daily active users. Shortly thereafter, Zynga opened studios in Los Angeles and Bangalore, India. Between 2010 and 2012, Zynga acquired or opened 18 offices in the United States, China, and Germany. Each office develops its own games. According to Kidd, Zynga operates like a federation of city-states, each with its own games run by autonomous teams. In 2010, it acquired both the Dallas-based Bonfire Studios and the mobile game developer Newtoys, Inc., developers of *Words with Friends* and *Chess with Friends*. When the company announced the purchase of video game maker Buzz Monkey in June 2012, along with their fifty-person Oregon office, it also acquired the very successful video games *Tomb Raider*, *Tony Hawk* and *FrontierVille*. Since its founding, Zynga has developed more than 30 popular games, accounting for 57 per cent of its revenues. With the acquisition of MarketZero, an online poker tracker company, it was able to launch in late 2012 Zynga Slingo, a knock-off of the popular slots bingo combination games found in casinos. Table 4.4 looks at the primary ways Pioneers stage their activities.

Table 4.4 Key Staging Issues for Pioneers
• First-to-market
• Run faster than competitors

Distinction

There is little doubt that the bedrock of any strategy is a firm's ability to distinguish itself from its rivals. For Pioneers, distinction stems primarily from the ability to identify and serve an unmet need in a way that established businesses have not been able to do thus far. Distinction rests on an organizational capability to continue generating new ideas that result in valuable, sought-after products. In other words, having a wonderful concept or idea by itself is insufficient to stay distinctive; the Pioneer must translate that idea into a desired, profitable product and follow through. Sustaining distinction requires the Pioneer to take steps that make it difficult for like-minded competitors to easily enter their market, or to imitate their products. This means that Pioneers must continue to keep their new product pipelines full with improved offerings and even newer innovations. Often, this means spending up to 35 per cent of revenues on research and development (R&D). Even with this expenditure in mind, Pioneers will also face competitive challenges from other like-minded Pioneers as well as counterattacks from larger, better-funded established businesses.

Consider, for example, the meteoric rise of the social media businesses Foursquare and Groupon. Both companies aim to help businesses learn more about their customers and to offer special, time-limited promotions by sending either rewards or coupons through smartphone-generated messages. Yet, both firms may face real dangers from potent competitors who can readily imitate their offerings. In fact, both Foursquare and Groupon are beginning to face off against one another in the digital coupon arena. Originally conceived as a way for friends to check in and connect with each other, Foursquare developed smartphone apps that would enable users to earn "badges" that they can use with businesses who offer special promotions. Foursquare users can "follow" a company and acquire promotions from them when they click in or check in at certain times. Foursquare developed a free platform that enables businesses to create and refine special promotions using data gathered on customers who use the service in their search for specials.[13]

Groupon works with local businesses to arrange special discounts and one-off offers through virtual coupons that customers pay for in order to receive, for example, 50 per cent off the regular price of a product or service. When customers purchase the coupon, Groupon in turn splits the revenue from the customer with the retailer. Groupon hopes to sign up more participating retailers by offering them a kind of downside protection: there will be no "deal of the day" for that retailer unless a significant proportion of customers sign up by paying for the coupon. Those customers who did pay for the deal receive their money back.

While both ideas are novel, numerous competitors have already begun to swarm in, especially on Groupon's business model. There are dozens, if not hundreds, of similar sites that offer promotions to customers visiting different businesses, including Foursquare itself. Some of these new competitors include another social media site, LivingSocial, which has set its sights on doing many of the same things as Groupon. LivingSocial has reportedly received a major investment from Amazon. Google, for its part, may become a direct competitor to Groupon after its initial failure to purchase the company in 2010.

In this vastly expanding arena of social media-oriented businesses, the barriers to entry and exit so far remain few, and it is difficult for a Pioneer to sustain its distinctive offerings in the wake of numerous imitators. In fact, a new threat confronting both Foursquare and Groupon is the growing capability of established firms who are now adapting their email advertisements to send text messages to customers who shop in selected stores. Known as "geofencing," this process allows stores to implant sensors in strategic physical locations in order to offer virtual coupons to customers on their smartphones. Texting and virtual coupons have helped some supermarket chains enhance their customers' shopping experience, as shopping lists are automatically updated with the location of the specific food item in the exact aisle and shelf space.[14]

We are also witnessing another arena where Pioneers have created an entirely new way of serving customers' needs, but where it has become difficult for any of the start-up firms to build and sustain a strong competitive advantage. Consider the rise of a small company known as Square in 2010. Square introduced a new way for anyone (e.g., household help, taxicab drivers, students, sellers at antique shows and flea markets) to accept credit cards via their smartphones. Square developed a magnetic card-swipe technology that users can insert into their phone's audio earphone jack. This innovation immediately converted the phone into a credit-card processor that greatly enhanced a person's ability to sell merchandise and services to customers who prefer to go light on cash. For a small fee per transaction, Square dramatically enlarged the emerging market acceptance of digital cash. There are no other set-up or monthly costs, and even the stripe reader is free. Since its introduction, over two million people have become avid Square users. However, the system's technology and appeal have attracted numerous market entrants, including such larger firms as Intuit and PayPal. Both established firms are charging lower fees than Square's $2.75 per transaction. In addition, other smaller start-up firms are entering the same arena.[15]

To stay ahead of other aggressive new entrants, Square has recently introduced a new service called "Pay With Square," which enables customers to pay with their voice and the use of GPS systems embedded in their smartphones and the merchant's iPad devices. Customers must be willing to share the face photos associated with their credit cards and link up both with the Square system. Once entered, all customers need to do is announce who they are to the merchant. The merchant in turn enters the amount the customer purchases, and there are no signatures, paper bills, or other hassle. Of course, the customer loses a degree of privacy with this cashless digital payment system. The merchant is able to track clients through the use of GPS systems. However, Square is likely to face a new technology arms race from other Pioneers and established businesses who seek to carve out a market position in this fast-changing arena.[16]

Over time, Pioneers will find it hard to sustain their distinction in the wake of constant competitive challenges. In another arena, the entry of numerous web-based travel reservation sites over the past several years shows how difficult it can be to erect barriers to entry and imitation. Pioneers need to continue to invest in newer product concepts, better designs, advanced technologies, or proprietary sources of knowledge (e.g., patents, methods, techniques) that slow down competitor imitation. Even with a rich product pipeline, the Pioneer must execute and follow through on its innovations before other firms seize the idea and the initiative away from it.

As revamping the United States' transportation infrastructure becomes a more urgent short-term need, many firms are experimenting with new kinds of materials and construction techniques that can replace aging bridges and roads without the need for constant seasonal maintenance and periodic reconstruction. Concrete and steel structures provide for highway strength and stability, but roads deteriorate with temperature changes and the constant pounding of cars and trucks. Axion International, a small New Jersey-based science firm, is attempting to replace reinforcing steel with advanced recycled plastics to provide even greater structural strength. Tapping into research conducted with Rutgers University, Axion is molding steel structures by combining shredded plastic soda bottles and other disposables with fiberglass filaments. A high-temperature furnace then molds the compound into desired structural shapes that are the basis for small bridges and other applications. Axion's technology could find widespread uses into arenas once customers realize how much durability is built into the new materials.[17]

ViewCast is a $11 million company that develops industry-leading hardware and software for the transformation and delivery of professional quality video over broadband and mobile networks. Its products are used for a variety of audio and video communication applications, including corporate communications, security, training, conferencing, and broadcast applications. It competes with Digital Rapids, V-Brick, Inlet, and Envivio in this market—all of whom have sales less than $50 million. Broadcasting firms, such as the BBC, Fox, and ABC, use ViewCast products because of their reliability, automation, and scalability. ViewCast markets and sells its video products and services directly to end users, including Cisco Systems and Yahoo!, or through indirect distributors and resellers. ViewCast offers high-quality digital encoding solutions to a portion of the overall digital media value chain. Research and development expenses account for more than 27 per cent of its revenues. These expenses fluctuate depending upon factors such as the number of product introductions planned and new prototypes in the pipeline. The critical sources of distinction for Pioneers are found in Table 4.5.

Economic Logic

The economic logic of Pioneers rests on their ability to stay ahead of rivals—both existing and those likely to surface in the near future. Because of low entry and exit barriers, Pioneers must continue to invest and innovate for the future. Yet, the cash flow needed for continuous experimentation and sustained investment keeps Pioneers on the financial precipice. At Zynga, to bring a complete game to market can cost $1 million or more, and take months to design, beta-test, and then launch on Facebook. In an ideal world, profitability for Pioneers would stem from their first-mover advantage, including the ability to charge a premium price for their novel offerings. To the extent that the product idea takes off, Pioneers can become profitable by licensing their concept to more established firms seeking to enter the market themselves. A proprietary process or technique could also help Pioneers preserve some of their first-mover advantages, especially if established firms were unable to quickly circumvent or innovate a competing technology on their own.

Table 4.5 Ways to Achieve Distinction for Pioneers

- Develop novel, unique products
- Create a lasting image in customers' minds
- Offer superior quality
- Stay niche-focused
- Retain key talent

Pioneers can sometimes erect important switching costs for their buyers, particularly if the product or technology defines an industry-leading standard that captures an important market share. During the late 1980s and 1990s, for example, Apple was able to achieve many benefits from its fiercely loyal customer base that cherished its Macintosh operating system, a standard that remains the preferred choice for legions of people engaged in advertising, publishing, and other creative activities. In today's Internet-driven marketplace, both Google and Facebook created the leading technical standards for search engine and social networking technologies respectively. Yet, it remains to be seen whether new unforeseen rivals can transform this hypercompetitive landscape again.

For most Pioneers, external sources of funding remain essential to viability. Pioneers can survive only to the extent they possess a capability to rapidly commercialize their innovations and delay competitor imitation for as long as possible. This means that Pioneers must secure a steady stream of royalties and other payments generated and protected by strong proprietary features. Pioneers often gain the necessary financial support from private financiers or venture capitalists. Unless the product has the necessary proprietary features, financiers will not back it.

Strategic Discipline: R&D to Generate Ideas and Products

At the heart of the "guiding logic" of Pioneers is their riveting focus on fostering and sustaining new product ideas and concepts. Equally important, Pioneers must also execute by commercializing the idea into real products that customers want. Pioneers thrive by engaging in break-through ideas and products. Yet, it is important to recognize that being the first with a new product or technology does not automatically translate into a sustainable competitive advantage. Patents, copyrights, proprietary processes, and methods do not translate into competitive strength without the requisite, disciplined focus on execution as well. *A great technology does not equal a great business.* If there is anything that we learned from the past 30 years, it is that the most successful businesses are those that aim to keep their product offerings relevant to their customers while sustaining a high rate of innovation.

With highly flexible, organic structures, entrepreneurial cultures, and few manufacturing capabilities, these firms can accelerate the pace and scope of product innovations. By their very nature (mostly founded by entrepreneurs), they are risk-takers. Their unique insight, experiences, and product-driven capabilities allow them to translate a certain idea or opportunity into a new product. Yet, tightly adhering to this strategic discipline generates its own set of potential challenges.

First, Pioneers tend to focus on leading-edge technologies or market niches whose ultimate potential are unknown. Thus, they face the risk of technological overkill. Pioneers may find themselves refining a technology beyond the point (and cost) that meet the needs of customers or firms. Excessive zeal in pushing a technological concept may actually alienate a customer because of the design's growing complexity or unwieldiness. For example, when RCA first introduced digital video laser disks in the 1960s (the precursors of today's DVDs), the technological complexity surrounding their use in the home dissuaded customers from purchasing a large, cumbersome device that was prone to mechanical breakdown. Likewise, early word processing systems from the likes of Xerox and Wang required the user to learn intricate software-based instructions and to save data on huge floppy disks that made typing papers more difficult than it had been to date using traditional electric typewriters.

Because most Pioneers are young and small, they are also unable to dedicate the resources to monitor highly intricate accounting, human resources, marketing and other "infrastructure" tasks. Patents and proprietary processes may represent a Pioneer's economic assets in a balance-sheet sense, but it is the human capital that creates, sustains, and follows through on the Pioneer's innovations. Many Pioneer firms are highly dependent on venture capital or external funding from the established firms that are their alliance partners to sustain their growth. Leadership in Pioneer firms is highly dependent on a singularly focused CEO who may become overly wedded to a particular idea, product format, or design at the risk of ignoring more productive alternatives. Likewise, the Pioneer can face strategic overextension if the CEO develops a "Napoleon complex" and seeks to expand into too many arenas without sufficient understanding of customers and appropriate execution.

Pioneers depend on the CEO's cultivating of organizational designs that promote fast learning, experimentation, and encouragement of internal debate. Because many Pioneers license their technologies to other firms, they must also be able to use these strategic alliances as vehicles to better understand market developments and customer evolution. Pioneers are unlikely to possess all of the critical building blocks of an effective business on their own. For example, before it linked up with Facebook, Zynga did not have a vehicle with which to market its games. Pioneers are particularly attractive acquisition candidates for established firms seeking to learn and to build entirely new core competencies, as Procter & Gamble did with Chicopee Mills, and Miller Brewing did with Gablinger's, the original brewer of light beer. However, they often represent a difficult cultural and organizational fit with the management practices and routines that are embedded in an established firm's organization. Thus, judicious decision-making is needed about the optimal degree of integration between established firms and Pioneers. For example, when telecommunications equipment and networking giant Cisco Systems acquired Inlet, a Pioneer that possessed an emerging but promising technology, Cisco recognized the value in preserving Inlet's human capital and frequently unconventional culture to encourage the kind of innovative thinking needed to push the cutting edge. Cisco pays its newly acquired talent lavishly and gives them considerable autonomy to develop their technology using all the existing resources (e.g., distribution, supply chain, accounting) that it already has in place. Over time, the Pioneer's talent will take on important management roles throughout Cisco as their technology blossoms and matures.

Pathways to Advantage and Avoiding the Entrepreneurial Graveyard

Once they create a winning product concept, successful Pioneers are often acquisition candidates for established firms seeking to enter a new market or technology arena. For example, the digital animation firm Pixar, which created the breakthrough technologies behind technically advanced special effects films such as *Toy Story*, set the standard for ever more realistic animation and science fiction films. Its success led to its eventual acquisition by the Walt Disney Company. Likewise, in the pharmaceutical industry, many firms—including Merck, Glaxo Smith Kline, Pfizer, and Bristol-Myers Squibb—are constantly on the lookout for Pioneering biotechnology and genomic firms that offer the potential for breakthrough therapies and genetic-decoding algorithms that can open the path to new disease cures. General Electric, Intel, Pfizer, Microsoft, and Cisco Systems are just a few of the many large firms that hope to gain access to new product concepts and technologies developed by start-up Pioneers. In particular, GE looks to start-ups as a way to boost its own R&D investments. In 2011, GE invested in 20 small ventures, especially in the alternative energy industry. It launched a $300 million fund together with energy giants NRG Energy and ConocoPhilips to pursue deals with small energy start-ups. Also, GE committed $40 million to eSolar, which uses solar energy to power steam turbines,[18] in order to learn more about solar-thermal energy conversion technology.

Across many high-technology sectors, start-up firms with promising ideas and technologies rapidly become targets for venture capitalists seeking to capitalize on a Pioneer's potential breakthrough. For example, start-up software companies routinely receive funding from external investors hoping to ride along with a new technology's trajectory. Many software companies are now looking at ways to make, convert, and improve traditional business transactions using application-like software to lower processing costs and to improve mobility. Some of these technologies apply social-media networking algorithms and techniques to enhance faster, real-time communications among managers and workers, no matter their location: both Jive Software and Yammer offer new types of software that enable companies to build and manage their own social networks. Yammer is also working on a micro-blogging and social-networking service specifically for business customers. Both companies have received funding from venture capitalists over the past few years.[19]

Evolution of Pioneers

Some very successful Pioneers are ultimately able to compete on their own. By enhancing their organization's fast-innovation capabilities, many Pioneers become Trendsetters or Consolidators as they develop sustainable competitive advantages. For example, Apple's own proud legacy began with a Pioneering concept (the original PC from the late 1970s) that enabled it to hone the leading-edge design skills that it uses to dominate many segments of today's consumer electronics industry. Another successful Pioneer that has become a Trendsetter in its own right is Priceline, which has established itself as the leading travel website where consumers can negotiate the prices they pay for airline tickets, hotel rooms, and car rentals. Over time, other Pioneers become Consolidators. Witness the steady growth of Amgen, a leading biotechnology drug firm, which started in Silicon Valley as a small venture capital start-up. In recent years, Amgen has begun acquiring other drug companies (e.g., Immunex) to build critical mass in its rheumatoid arthritis and septic drug treatment pipelines.

Avoiding the Entrepreneurial Graveyard

Every business, of course, confronts its own set of risks and dangers. Pioneers certainly face challenges from every direction—competitive pressures from other start-ups, entrance by established firms into the Pioneer's arenas, imitation of the Pioneer's distinctive offerings, outright encroachment or theft of the Pioneer's intellectual property in some cases, and the simple fact that cash dries up faster than anyone previously anticipated. Yet, there is one overriding theme that dominates Pioneers' strategic considerations. As noted above, *a great technology does not automatically mean a great business.* Breakthrough technology by itself has no economic value whatsoever unless it is translated into a product desired by customers who are willing to pay for it. Often, the companies that create radically new products are not necessarily those that succeed in the mass market. Pioneers are rarely able to create an organization capable of exploiting new technologies quickly enough to serve the mass market, and thus wind up in the entrepreneurial graveyard.

When most people think about ordering books online, they probably think that Amazon invented the business. In fact, the genesis of the idea originated with Charles Stack, an Ohio-based bookseller in 1991.

Amazon, under CEO Jeff Bezos, did not enter the market until 1995. Likewise, when one thinks about who pioneered the first safety shaving razor? The natural answer would be Gillette, but in reality, the first safety razor was created by Henry Gaisman, founder of the AutoStrop Safety Razor Corporation in 1928. In 1930, Gillette bought AutoStrop and its safety razor patent. These examples highlight a key point. Frequently, the companies that create radically new products are not necessarily those that succeed in the mass market. For example, Xerox is widely credited with having created in the early 1960s Ethernet technology, the basis for today's Internet. Xerox is also credited with having invented the graphical user interface (GUI), the basis for today's easy-to-use icons in software operating systems. However, Xerox's excellence in blue-sky research across a variety of scientific fields did not translate into competitive success for any major consumer electronics product. Even Xerox's core copiers did not use Ethernet for anything other than connecting computers to copiers in an office environment. Pioneers are rarely able to create an organization capable of exploiting new technologies quickly enough to serve the mass market, and thus wind up in the entrepreneurial graveyard.

The first-mover advantages that Pioneers enjoy also bring with them important strategic disadvantages. The Pioneer's investment in R&D and marketing also has the effect of signaling to the market that customers can expect a constant flow of new products. However, other start-ups and established firms can now take advantage of the information from the Pioneer's efforts to create their own version of the Pioneer's offering. By "free-riding" off the Pioneer's information, marketing, and even its missteps, the firms that rapidly follow the Pioneer can offer their own product versions at lower cost than that of the Pioneer. The opportunity to piggy-back off a Pioneer's innovation poses a constant challenge that is difficult to prevent and defend. Effectively, the Pioneer ultimately does much of the "work" and takes all of the risk in reducing the technological uncertainty that fast followers face when commercializing new products for customers. Fast followers can see what particular attributes customers are willing to pay for, and adjust their own product developments efforts accordingly—all without the upfront risk that the

Pioneer faced when it started out. Fast followers who enter a market after a technological standard or product design is established face much lower risks that the Pioneers who created them. The strategic vulnerabilities of Pioneers are found in Table 4.6.

Sustaining Pioneer Viability

There are several implications for Pioneers. First, new products do not automatically translate into a successful business model without a supporting organizational design that promotes and sustains fast innovation. Initial products frequently do not satisfy a well-articulated need; therefore, adoption rates are often slow. To survive, Pioneers must have a deep knowledge of their product ideas, strong financial backing, and be interested in pushing its cutting-edge capabilities. These firms are serial risk-takers because they are willing to bet on the results of new products that extend beyond the existing state of knowledge.

Second, Pioneers need to create flat management systems so they can quickly respond to the developments of cutting-edge technologies. Learning new technological skills and information is prized and rewarded. Their competitive advantage stems from their ability to remain flexible and agile to hit a moving target. Customers of Pioneers often share an enthusiasm for the new concept, and Pioneers must seek to learn from their customers what they truly want from the company's offering.

Third, effective Pioneers must be ready to leap into a new market which the established firms have largely ignored in favor of their own familiar turf. Since Pioneers do not have the capabilities and "infrastructure" necessary to compete in mature markets, they should spend

Table 4.6 Perils of Pioneers

- Cash/credit drives up
- CEO's ego overshadows organization
- Arrival of substitute technology
- Key talent leaves

their time developing and refining new product ideas that bypass what older firms are doing.

The annals of business history are replete with examples of bold pioneering firms that ultimately misjudged the market's acceptance of their breakthrough idea or products and ended up in the entrepreneurial graveyard as a result. In many cases, the pioneering firm either runs into stiff competition or depletes its scarce cash resources. Pioneering firms in particular need continuous injections and flows of cash to keep their visions, product ideas, and technologies alive. All too often, however, when the cash is depleted, so is the Pioneer's time to commercialize its idea. Steve Jobs' promotion of Lisa at Apple Computer in the early 1980s, Edwin Land's vision for Polaroid cameras, and Fred Smith's "zap mail" at Federal Express (now FedEx) were all major technological projects that customers eventually rejected. Likewise, the rise of People Express, a no-frills, low-cost airline in the early 1980s, initially attracted widespread acclaim from eager passengers who were thrilled to be paying a fraction of the fares charged for air travel at the time. People Express offered standardized pricing for its flights, but actually initiated the practice of charging for checked-in luggage. Yet, People Express ran into significant funding difficulties as it sought to rapidly expand to major cities throughout the United States. As it did so, the company began to adopt some of the practices of the better known airlines, such as offering first-class seating and higher fares for business travelers. Consequently, People Express exhibited many of the characteristics of the legacy carriers, as growing labor difficulties, a heavy debt burden, and a brutal competitive response from established airlines finally forced the airline to sell itself to Trans-Texas Air Corporation in 1987. Trans-Texas Air is the predecessor of today's Continental Airlines.

Cash Flow Dries Up

Until they commercialize a value product, Pioneers survive solely on the cash they raise; this comes primarily from external sources and from the founder(s) themselves. It is a matter of time before all Pioneers ultimately need to raise cash, often successively before a viable business model takes root. Consider the experience of Silicon Valley start-up Tabula,

Inc., which has pioneered a new way of designing programmable logic chips that customers can use to perform specific technical tasks once the chips leave the factory. Tabula has created a new technology that partitions logic instructions into multiple sets that are loaded onto chips in successive waves, thereby allowing the industrial end-user to accomplish much larger complex tasks faster than they would do using more expensive chips. In March 2011, Tabula gained a $108 million infusion from several venture capital firms to keep its operations going. This latest round of funding means that external investors have contributed upwards of $214 million into the company. One of the venture investors notes that with such an ambitious technology, it often takes longer than expected to translate the idea into a workable product.[20]

The roller-coaster ride and the ultimate bankruptcy of A123 Systems, a small developer of advanced electric vehicle batteries, reveals the tenuous financial position that Pioneers face. After having already received upwards of $249 million from the U.S. Department of Energy, A123 ploughed the money to build an advanced battery plant in Michigan. Customers' initial receptivity to the company's battery technology proved lukewarm, and the plant was underused as a result. In addition, A123 sustained significant financial losses as a result of poor manufacturing quality in some of its earliest battery variants, forcing an expensive recall to fix the defects. Cash eventually dried up as A123's technology development efforts consumed ever more resources. In February 2013, the U.S. government gave its approval for China-based Wanxiang Group to purchase A123 Systems for $257 million, despite some initial political resistance to the idea of a Chinese firm buying a U.S. firm that possesses leading-edge technology.[21]

The phoenix-like renaissance of Eclipse Aerospace reveals just how volatile the Pioneer's competitive and funding environment can become. Eclipse Aerospace is the reincarnation of Eclipse Aviation, which filed for bankruptcy in 2008, despite having received funding from Microsoft co-founder Bill Gates. At the time, Eclipse Aviation developed a series of ultra-small passenger jets that competed with the likes of Canada's Bombardier and Brazil's Embraer. Unfortunately for Eclipse, the confluence of the 2008 credit crisis-inspired market downturn, combined with rapid entry by Textron's Cessna unit, Diamond Aircraft, and Honda, conspired to put Eclipse out of business. Although it hoped to gear up high-volume production from a state-of-the-art plant in Albuquerque, Eclipse was just not able to beat the lower cost offerings of the more established small aircraft firms already in business. One of Eclipse's biggest customers at the time was DayJet, a firm that aspired to run an air-taxi business in Florida. It, too, became a victim of the 2008 downturn.

Now, Eclipse Aerospace has redefined its original aircraft design to become much more fuel-efficient. The company now hopes to sell the aircraft to charter operators, individual aircraft owners, and even the government for its use as training aircraft and special operations. With a recent $25 million investment from the Sikorsky aircraft unit of United Technologies, Eclipse has outsourced key elements of aircraft production to lower-cost venues (e.g., a Sikorsky subsidiary in Poland) to streamline its predecessor's far-flung and cumbersome supply chain. To recapture its customer base, the newest models will be able to fly in the ice and come equipped with automatic speed control as well as GPS systems.[22]

Consider the meteoric rise and fall of the pioneering aviation firm DayJet, which purchased its aircraft from the aforementioned Eclipse Aviation! Founded in 2002, DayJet was a start-up that attempted to commercialize the idea of providing an "air taxi" service. Having plans to eventually order some 300 planes from Eclipse Aviation, DayJet intended to operate an air service using aircraft that seated only between two and five people. Its CEO, Ed Iacobucci, envisioned this service as a shared ride service in the air. Focusing on smaller cities that the larger airlines have ignored or abandoned, DayJet began serving smaller Florida cities in October 2007 and had ambitions to serve medium-sized cities in 2008. Even though Iacobucci knew he could not directly compete with the established airline firms, DayJet overextended its capital by planning to order so many planes from Eclipse Aviation. By September 2008, with the exacerbation of the global credit crisis, DayJet ceased operations. DayJet misjudged the dynamics of the industry, thus rendering their capabilities worthless.

An Uncontrolled CEO's Ego

The CEO's vision, sweat equity, personal funding, and leadership skills are essential for the Pioneer's inception and survival. His or her strong leadership skills can provide the continuous inspiration needed to motivate a dedicated cadre of technical personnel and employees to continue experimenting, innovating, and creating new products, even if the risks of failure are high. Yet, strong CEOs can sometimes be a mixed blessing for the Pioneer's organization. Sometimes, they may become so maniacally dedicated to their vision that they ignore the vital building blocks necessary to sustain a business. For example, the father of light beer, Dr. James Owades, entered the brewing trade by inventing a process to eliminate starch from beer. His process resulted in a "light" beer that had significantly fewer calories and carbohydrates than regular beers. Introducing his new product as Gablinger's Diet Beer in 1967, Dr. Owades focused solely on improving the fermentation process behind the light beer, and ignored other critical business activities such as marketing, financing, and advertising. Ultimately, Dr. Owades shared his formula with a friend at another brewery, which in turn was purchased by Miller Brewing. Miller coined the memorable phrase "tastes great, less filling" and used its nationwide distribution power to chalk up enormous market share gains during the 1980s.[23]

In other cases, CEOs may be so consumed with their vision that their firms begin to overextend their operations and diversify into too many arenas, none of which ultimately is distinctive. Consider the rapid growth of RCA during the middle part of the previous century. Under its legendary genius CEO, David Sarnoff, RCA played an important role in either inventing or developing key products that we now take for granted—radio transmission, television transmission, color television, digital laser discs, video recording, and other major electronic product landmarks. Although RCA was a small part of General Electric in its earliest years, young Sarnoff proved himself a technical genius when he helped commercialize the first practical radio. After GE was compelled to divest RCA, Sarnoff became its president and CEO. Yet, Sarnoff's fierce belief in pursuing cutting-edge research produced a flood of patents and innovations that became integral to every aspect of electronics, communications, and broadcasting. However, Sarnoff's scientific zeal afforded RCA the opportunity to enter into a variety of scientific disciplines (some of which bore little relationship to RCA's products). This resulted in difficulties for the electronics giant when it could not compete with emerging Japanese electronics firms entering the U.S. market in the 1960s and 1970s.

Fast forward to the 1980s, and you have the story of Oprah Winfrey's meteoric rise from a broadcast news reporter to a multi-billionaire whose long-running television show and production company create a new series of programs to help millions of women seek new joy and revitalized health in their lives. In 2010, Winfrey decided to exit from her wildly successful afternoon talk show to create her own television and media production company. The Oprah Winfrey Network (OWN) is half-owned by Discovery Communications. However, her first two years in the business proved to be a rough road, as running a television network is very different from hosting a daytime television show. Winfrey began learning about the ins and outs of working and selling to cable companies, satellite companies, subscription fees, advertising rates, network program scheduling, and other financial details that make or break an entertainment company. Although greatly admired by her mostly female viewers, Winfrey casts a major shadow over the operation and has an effective veto over what Discovery Communications can recommend or suggest to improve OWN's viability.

Business history is full of examples where maniacal CEOs make decisions that ultimately ruin their businesses. Consider the following excerpt from *The Washington Post*:[24]

> History offers many other examples of self-destructive CEOs: Ed Land of Polaroid, Ken Olsen of Digital Equipment, William Black of Chock Full O'Nuts, Juan Trippe of Pan American World Airlines and Dick Fuld of the reborn Lehman Brothers, to name a few. Land held 533 patents, second only to Thomas Edison as an inventor, but could not accept the emergence of new imaging and video technologies, and Polaroid lost its innovative edge. Olsen

created the world's second-largest computer company but failed to capitalize on the shift to personal computing. The original coffee-house chain with branded premier coffee, Chock Full O'Nuts, was led by Black for 61 years — including the last two, 1981–83, when he was incapacitated at Massachusetts General Hospital.

Arrival of Substitute Technology

Even the most promising business ideas will always face the threat of competitor imitation and substitute technology. In the last few years, perhaps the most powerful example of a Pioneer attaining mythical status and then landing with quite a thud is MySpace. Founded in 2003 and subsequently acquired three years later by News Corporation for close to $600 million, MySpace was the most used and viewed social networking site for several years—it even surpassed Google in the number of visits in 2006. By 2008, however, Facebook had already overtaken MySpace and the company has grown increasingly irrelevant ever since. Recently, News Corporation sold its investment for $35 million to personal investors.

The electronics business is replete with numerous examples of where a Pioneer introduces a cutting-edge concept, only to see its investment overshadowed by a better and more powerful competitor's offerings. Go far back as the 1970s, and one sees how Ampex, a leading U.S. electronics firm that developed core technology sound and video recording capabilities, loses its grasp over the video recording business to Japan's Sony. Ampex pioneered the first video recording device back in 1956, and its standard became the basis for broadcasters worldwide. Ampex's breakthrough technology enabled television stations to transmit pre-recorded broadcasts and commercials. The company even won Emmys and Academy Awards for technical achievement. Some of its core patents are still considered essential cornerstones for today's video technology. However, Sony, under Akio Morita, developed a much superior method to recording video broadcasting through a cassette format (Betamax) that proved much easier to use and more durable than Ampex's reel-to-reel. Sony continued to invest in state-of-the-art research and manufacturing to further refine and improve the acceptance of Betamax and its use in both commercial and household recording. Interestingly enough, despite its own legendary innovation prowess, the Japanese giant found itself caught in a similar bind when Matsushita Electric (now known as Panasonic) and JVC created an alternative video cassette format known as VHS. By harnessing strong original-equipment manufacturing (OEM) relationships with American and European firms that chose to outsource VCR manufacturing, Matsushita was able to outflank and eventually overcome Sony's VCR dominance, despite the superiority of Sony's format and first-mover advantage in cassette technology.

Key Human Capital Leave

We have previously identified some of the issues that place Pioneers in the entrepreneurial graveyard. Pioneers face an existential threat when key personnel, especially the creative minds, leave the organization. A Pioneer that illustrates an overlay of these problems is Stage Stores, the retail chain created by Bain Capital in 1988. In a decade, the outlet grew sales from $400 million to over $1.1 billion. Stage's strategy was to target chains primarily located in smaller Texas markets that did not have many fashion-based retailers. It wanted to be the dominant local retailer, like a soft-goods version of Wal-Mart. To fuel this growth, Stage relied heavily on debt to fuel its acquisitions and growth. In 1996, Stage Stores went public and used its cash to pay down that debt. Then in 1997, Staged acquired C. R. Reynolds, another retailing chain with more than 300 outlets in New Mexico, Oklahoma, Louisiana, and Texas. The acquisition proved difficult to integrate because of different retailing approaches. Several key merchandising managers left, and Carl Tooker, Stage Stores' first CEO, resigned shortly thereafter. Bain Capital subsequently cashed out of the stores. The loss of key human capital, along with important financial support, led to bankruptcy in 2000. According to Tooker, "It was a success then became a failure because we grew outside of our comfort zone."[25]

MASTERING THE ESSENTIALS OF A PIONEER

Mastering the essentials of a pioneer involves:

- translating a vision into an actionable mission;
- satisfying an unmet customer need;
- embracing risk and challenging the status quo;
- securing the cash and credit lifelines of the business;
- attracting and developing key resources;

and avoiding the following:

- the CEO or founder's ego overshadowing activities;
- cash flow or credit lines drying up;
- product features overkill;
- key talent leaving.

Notes

1 Mark Kurlansky, *Birdseye: The Adventures of a Curious Man*, Doubleday, New York, 2012.
2 Taken from the Frito-Lay website, http://www.fritolay.com/about-us/history.html.
3 From the Nestlé website, http://www.hotpockets.com/aboutus/index.aspx.
4 See "From Brazil to a Full Plate in Texas," *The Dallas Morning News*, July 24, 2011, pp. 1D, 10D.
5 See "The Man Behind the Commodore 64," *Wall Street Journal*, April 10, 2012, p. B6.
6 See "The Man Who Knows What's Next," *Wired*, May 2012, pp. 162–169.
7 An exceptional academic work that examines the notion of first-mover advantage is M. Lieberman and C. Montgomery, "First-Mover Advantages," *Strategic Management Journal*, Volume 9, 1988, pp. 41–58.
8 Richard Branson, *Losing My Virginity*, Crown Business, New York, 2007, p. 77.
9 See "Supercharged," *Wired*, October 2012, pp. 139–180.
10 See "A David and Gillette Story," *Wall Street Journal*, April 11, 2012, pp. B1, B8.
11 See *Fast Company*, March 2011, pp. 85–86, 132.
12 Emily Ross and Angus Holland, "Dyson: Suck It and See," *100 Great Businesses and the Minds Behind Them*, Sourcebooks, Naperville, IL, 2006, pp. 40–44.
13 See "Foursquare Joins the Coupon Craze," *Wall Street Journal*, May 8, 2012, pp. B1, B9.
14 See "Can Texting Save Stores," *Wall Street Journal*, May 8, 2012, pp. B1, B9.
15 See "The Death of Cash," *Fortune*, July 23, 2012, pp. 118–129.
16 See "Pay By Voice? So Long Wallet," *The New York Times*, July 18, 2012.
17 See "Bottles to Bridges," *Forbes*, April 30, 2012, p. 35.
18 See "GE's Big Bet on Small Firms," *Wall Street Journal*, September 11, 2011, p. R2.
19 See "Software From Big Tech Firms, Start-Ups Takes Page from Facebook," *Wall Street Journal*, March 29, 2011, p. B7.

20 See "Chip Firm Gains Sizable Infusion," *Wall Street Journal*, March 28, 2011, p. B7.
21 See "Battery Firm Sees Loss, Plans Debt Offering," *Wall Street Journal*, May 14, 2012, p. B2. Also, "China Steps Up Buying in the U.S.," *Wall Street Journal*, February 9, 2013, p. A1.
22 See "Tiny Jet Plans a Big Comeback," *Wall Street Journal*, July 11, 2012, pp. B1, B2.
23 See "Joseph Owades Dies at 86, The Father of Light Beer," *The Washington Post*, December 31, 2005.
24 See J. Sonnenfeld, "Analysis: Facebook Board Must Deal with Genius CEO," *The Washington Post*, May 2012.
25 See D. Michaels, "Texas Retail Stake Paid Off for Bain," *The Dallas Morning News*, July 22, 2012, pp. A1, A25.

5
TRENDSETTERS

Firms create and offer a seemingly endless flow of innovative products and services designed to tantalize and delight their customers. In this chapter, we focus on Trendsetters—the businesses that define and raise the standards for the kind of value that customers should receive.

Competing in high-growth industries, Trendsetters strive to be unique in what they offer and are often synonymous with a distinctive way of doing things that also raises the bar for their rivals. Those pursuing a Trendsetter strategy continually tailor and shape their products and services to fit an increasingly precise definition of the customer. This can be costly, but Trendsetters are willing to spend resources to build customer loyalty and to innovate for the future. They typically look at the customer's long-term value to the business. If we take a broad sample of industries, we can see how Trendsetters have effectively shaped the competitive landscape and customer expectations in each one:

- Nintendo—video gaming systems;
- PetSmart—pet accessories, services, and family atmosphere;
- Nordstrom—personalized shopping experience;
- The Ritz-Carlton—exceptional service;
- The Container Store—knowledgeable staff;

- Dyson—constant new product innovation in cleaning appliances;
- Whole Foods Market—transforming what we eat.

Trendsetters live and breathe customer intimacy and innovation. Innovation can be focused around designing the best performance products, or delivering the highest level of customer intimacy to gain customer satisfaction. Trendsetters constantly experiment with new product and service concepts to see which ones work best. Constantly gathering and sorting through enormous reams of data, they educate and update themselves to determine how to create the best-in-class value proposition for their customers. Trendsetters are in the vanguard of shaping their customers' expectations, whether they be, for example, memorable shopping experiences for buying clothes (e.g., Nordstrom), entertaining (e.g., Nintendo's Wii gaming system), purchasing and maintaining cars (e.g., Sewell Automotive), or designing the technical standards for chips used in modern digital technology (e.g., Qualcomm chips in Samsung smartphones). Customer expectations require Trendsetters to stay agile and nimble so that they can respond quickly to new market segments, changing customer needs, and shifting technological trajectories. Excellence in everything that the Trendsetter does is the critical survival factor—want-to-be rivals lurk just around the corner, ready to pounce on even the smallest misstep. Likewise in today's digital age of Twitter and Facebook, customers can just as easily turn cold on a Trendsetter if they feel a loss of customer intimacy.

Trendsetters compete by designing business processes focused around setting the industry standard for performance. Trendsetters create a distinct—ideally unique—value proposition that attracts customers. Customer purchases, price points, feedback, repeat transactions, buying patterns, and usage patterns provide the data that lay the foundation for the Trendsetter's innovation-driven strategy. The data help the Trendsetter identify what it can do to create a defining, leading-edge standard in the industry. This is true for purchases of products and services made by individual consumers, as well as for commercial customers seeking the best technology solutions for their business needs. But this strategy is worthless if the Trendsetter cannot evaluate

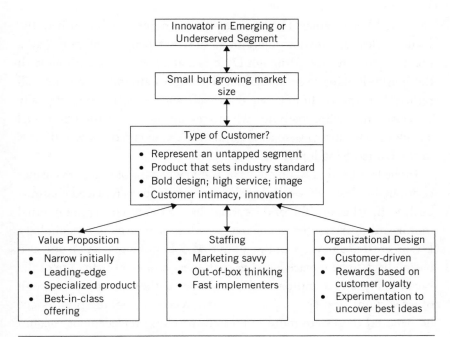

Figure 5.1 The Foundation of a Trendsetter.

and translate this data into clear, distinct priorities of what the business must do to continue satisfying the customer, be it the everyday consumer or a high-tech firm. Financial performance metrics are vital, but they represent the end result of a deeply rooted system of prioritized processes that deliver consistent and delightful results to customers time and again. This is true for both product and service businesses. As Carl Sewell of Sewell Automotive once wrote, it is all about "systems, not smiles."[1] Figure 5.1 presents the major elements of a Trendsetter's strategic and organizational approach.

Vacuum Cleaners, Containers, Hotel Stays, and Video Games

Dyson

Most people look at housecleaning chores as drudgery—especially vacuuming large rooms with a machine that was designed by engineers who probably cannot completely empathize with the person doing the cleaning. Meet James Dyson, a brilliant engineer, who turned the vacuum cleaner into an object of desire that people willingly pay a premium to purchase. Although Dyson's name is now synonymous with the quirky-looking vacuum cleaner that moves around on a giant ball rather than the traditional set of wheels and axles, Dyson originally conceived his rolling ball idea when seeking to replace the traditional wheels on wheelbarrows so as to not damage manicured lawns and yards in the United Kingdom.

In the late 1970s, Dyson grew frustrated when his old vacuum cleaner continued to lose suction and needed to have its bags replaced continuously as they became full of dust and debris. By redesigning the internal motor and dust-capturing apparatus with a new "cyclone" technology, Dyson created a new type of vacuum that does not lose suction and also has no bags to be replaced, saving customers money over the life of the vacuum. Dyson attempted to sell this state-of-the-art concept through other vacuum cleaner companies, only to receive a cool reception, since he believed they were more interested in selling replacement vacuum cleaner bags. His initial "cyclone" technology was sold under license exclusively in Japan as the G-Force, and its high-tech looks were a sensation.

In 1993, Dyson on his own rolled out his original DC-01 machine with a "dual cyclone" technology where people can actually watch the machine suck in the debris and dust into the machine. Although most appliance makers thought that customers would be turned off by such a sight, in reality, Dyson's machine became a hit because people enjoyed seeing the fruit of their labors. The high-tech, flamboyant machine soon became a fashion statement and looked far more appealing than standard machines offered by competitors. Dyson's distinctive rolling ball design, combined with his signature technology, has made his machines the high-tech gold standard for household vacuums. Dyson is also working on a series of revolutionary washing machine appliances, as well as electronic hand dryers, that also incorporate novel ideas to dramatically improve mundane cleaning tasks as well. Now, the Dyson name is fast becoming a global brand signifying leading-edge design.[2]

The Container Store

How has The Container Store thrived selling simple plastic containers, especially in the wake of fierce competition from much bigger retailers, such as Target and Wal-Mart Stores? Founded in 1978 by Garrett Boone and Kip Tindell, The Container Store now calls itself "The Original Storage and Organization Store" and has led the way of putting home storage solutions on the merchandising map. Although other retailing firms soon followed with their own home storage-based products, The Container Store continues to draw a remarkably dedicated following from customers who relish the company's wide variety of different solutions to storing everything from clothing to food to treasured family photos.

One of the company's core business philosophies is that employees should strive to work together with individual customers to find the best solution for their unique storage needs. Under the company approach called "Shelf Help," highly motivated employees are encouraged to develop a high level of customer intimacy with customers to generate ideas for custom-made solutions from a huge variety of different container sizes and uses. Most customers entering the store do not say they need a particular-sized hook, shelf, or container; instead, they often comment that they cannot fit their clothes in the closet or pack everything they want into their garage. Employees provide all kinds of advice (for free) and will even go so far as to plan the organization of their rooms, closets, or other space. Customers often leave The Container Store proud of their purchases and some even develop an emotional attachment to their storage products. For more challenging needs, The Container Store's personnel are even able to create customized adaptations of complex modular storage systems that are unique to each customer's closet size, configuration, and type of items being stored. Many of the ideas for constructing custom storage solutions are based on employees' previous experiences and new insights learned from other customers who shared a different storage challenge. The Container Store attempts to develop a high level of "empathy" with its customers to ensure that they receive the maximum economic and emotional value from their purchases.[3]

PetSmart

The United States' largest retailer of pet supply products is riding a new trend: people are beginning to treat their pets not as animals, but more like family members who deserve the best they can afford. PetSmart has opened one thousand stores since 2007 and has led the way in creating highly desired services, such as Doggie Day Care, luxurious pet lodging, and in-house veterinary services through its Banfield unit. As customers flock in to take advantage of these new services, PetSmart has launched its own line of premium, private-label products that now compose 23 per cent of its $6 billion revenues. CEO Bob Moran has navigated PetSmart to adopt a more local look for each store. Instead of selling the same line and types of products everywhere, the merchandise in each PetSmart store reflects the relative ratio of dogs to cats that live in the surrounding neighborhood. By adding new services, PetSmart is hoping to become a kind of pet-oriented Starbucks, where people come in to socialize with other pet owners, while looking at the increasingly upscale products offered (including natural and organic pet food).[4]

The Ritz-Carlton

The Ritz-Carlton luxury brand prides itself on creating a "mystique" that broadly captures the brand image, the unique ambience of each hotel, and the ultra-personalized treatment that each guest receives. Although Ritz-Carlton hotels are found in numerous locations around the world, the company encourages individual hotel properties to adapt to the needs of their customers according to the Ritz's highest levels of service standards. These service standards focus on delivering excellence at every level and point of customer contact, but they constantly evolve as the organization further refines its ambience and image. Behind The Ritz-Carlton "mystique" is an extreme, almost obsessive level of attention to detail in every aspect of each hotel's operations. According to senior management, the company gathers and analyzes every possible data point that employees monitor in their daily activities. This data is then used to continuously monitor processes and identify areas in immediate need of improvement.

Refining and enhancing The Ritz-Carlton's "mystique" presents a daily challenge that senior management sees as a way of deepening its relationship with its customers. Cross-functional teams composed of front-line employees, HR managers, marketing managers, and even senior corporate managers work together to sort through all of this data in order to design strategies that are best suited for each Ritz-Carlton location. This total reliance on employees to gather and communicate this data is extremely important to the company, as they are the eyes and ears of what customers want and need. These requirements can vary from one location to another. A big part of The Ritz-Carlton's success is the way that it teaches its employees to read customers' emotional signals, including body language and subtle nuances that may indicate a dislike or a hesitation. This information is converted into hard data that then enables employees and managers to identify the critical business priorities to which each hotel should devote itself if it wants to improve. Managers and employees are constantly learning new ways to develop strong ties to their customers, and to look at individual customers as potential sources of learning too.[5]

Nintendo

Nintendo is a company that has dramatically raised the bar in creating new types of video games that delight customers by encouraging them to move and spend time with their families. Unlike traditional video games that tend to foster kids' growing isolation from their parents and friends, Nintendo's Wii system encourages people of all ages to join in. Under the company's new slogan, "Wii would like you to play," Nintendo has created and expanded a new gaming market by innovating a simple and fun system that even encourages badly needed physical exercise. The Wii video game system includes such virtual games as tennis, golf, baseball, and boxing. Adults enjoy the Wii system as much as the kids. But Nintendo has not stopped there either: it has created another highly interactive gaming system known as the Nintendo DS that has attracted wide acclaim for an expanding number of games designed to help middle-aged adults sharpen their brain function and memory. Nintendo hopes that its DS-based games will even enable adult parents to reach the same mental and visual dexterity as that of their game-playing children.[6]

Strategic Issues Facing Trendsetters

Our examples reveal that Trendsetters can set and redefine customers' expectations in many industries. By offering a highly innovative value proposition that attracts customers' interest, Trendsetters often carve out entirely new product categories or market segments that exhibit very high growth rates. In many instances, Trendsetters in consumer-oriented markets become brand leaders. In industrial or commercial products, they often shape and set the standards that define a product design or technology. Despite the many economic differences that separate consumer and industrial markets, Trendsetters in both markets rely on their customers for continuous feedback of information and data to ensure that they meet their increasingly sophisticated or complex needs. This becomes especially important as lead customers in many industries become increasingly involved in co-creating and even co-designing products with firms.

Trendsetters attempt to build and sustain competitive advantage through constant innovation and customer intimacy. The innovation-driven imperative facing Trendsetters means that they must constantly explore for new opportunities to better serve customers, deepen their product expertise, or expand their operations. Staying abreast of future industry trends, evolving customer needs, and future technologies are tasks that all businesses need to do, but these are especially salient to Trendsetters as they look to deepen their customer relationships. This does not mean that Trendsetters are synonymous with businesses that seek a first-mover advantage—quite the contrary, in fact. Many successful Trendsetters are fast-followers who learn from the mistakes, product innovations, and customer experiences of other firms to better understand the market and customer needs. The success of Trendsetters always attracts rivals that attempt to outflank or outrace them in delivering the next better thing to the market, just as Four Seasons Hotels competes with The Ritz-Carlton in the premium luxury hotel segment, for example. Of course, some rivals will seek to undercut the Trendsetter's pricing to woo away its customers. To fend off ambitious rivals, Trendsetters must compete and offer compelling value along a number of dimensions. They have to communicate that the value and benefits customers receive cannot be traded off for lower prices.

Trendsetters build brand equity by closely identifying and meeting customer needs that can be highly specialized, on the leading edge, or where a high degree of personal attention or customization can greatly increase customer satisfaction. However, even Trendsetters offering highly specialized or leading-edge products must still cultivate a high degree of customer intimacy, too. In turn, loyal, satisfied customers enable the Trendsetter to erect strong barriers to imitation from rivals. For example, Trendsetters can thrive by providing highly specialized products and/or services that require sales staff and technical personnel with deep knowledge (e.g., Williams-Sonoma, Bass Pro Shops, Intuitive Surgical Systems). These knowledgeable employees support customers in every stage of their information-gathering, decision-making, warranties, potential after-sales service needs, and the ultimate choice of what to buy. It is difficult for competitors offering a broader product line to develop and cultivate this type of specialized knowledge. Other Trendsetters become influential players in their industry by identifying an unmet need and harnessing it to become the organization of choice for customers. Whole Foods Market recognized the growing health-consciousness of U.S. consumers and their desire to eat healthier foods without preservatives and artificial growth hormones. Tapping this need powered Whole Foods' strategy to dominate the market for organic foods. Likewise, in the esoteric high-tech world of semiconductors, ARM Holdings realized that smaller electronic devices need ever more powerful chips that do not drain battery power. Over the past ten years, ARM Holdings has become the gold standard of power-efficient microchips now found in all types of portable electronic appliances and smartphones. Table 5.1 highlights the major strategic issues facing Trendsetters.

When customers become increasingly jaded or disappointed with the service they receive from established providers, they are highly receptive to Trendsetters that can take something highly mundane and boring

Table 5.1 Key Strategic Issues for Trendsetters

- Earn customers' loyalty
- Adapt quickly to changing customer needs
- Set the industry standard for product/service quality
- Service spearheads marketing efforts

and refresh it so that it becomes exciting again. This is the secret formula behind billionaire Richard Branson's approach to creating Virgin Atlantic in order to challenge the stiff and rigid service that customers received from British Airways. It is also the secret behind The Container Store's enormous success over the past 30 years in providing all types of storage solutions, as well as that of Sewell Automotive in constantly raising the service bar for its automotive customers.

One company that has harnessed customer intimacy is Apple. A company that has consistently been rated as one of the most innovative companies in the world by popular business publications, Apple became the most valuable publicly held company in August 2012. It is not only famous for its line of iPods, iPhones, and iPads, but it is also the biggest music company in the world and actually consumes close to 4 per cent of the world's semiconductor production. Having just won a major patent suit against its arch-rival Samsung, Apple is well-poised to dominate the music, smartphone, and "apps" universes even further. And yet in 1997, Apple was on its back, dead in the water until it received a $150 million cash infusion from Microsoft, who wanted to avoid possible anti-trust litigation if its much smaller rival failed.

The company, its late leader Steve Jobs, its products, and its retail stores have become such cultural icons that even its corporate rivals are seeking to emulate the firm's methods to innovate and deliver the newest technologies to legions of customers waiting in long lines. The Apple brand has attained such a following that it is almost synonymous with customer zeal. While remaining the topic of countless magazine articles and several books,[7] Apple's methods for cultivating innovation and customer intimacy remain hard to imitate, perhaps because it is so willing to challenge the conventional wisdom of running a high-tech business at so many levels. We believe that a number of consistent themes emerge that have lead to Apple's success.

First, Apple's late CEO Steve Jobs took on the role of chief product designer himself for many of the company's products. He met with his senior product development managers at least once a week and kept raising the bar for even better performance. Jobs really believed that his legendary line of Mac computers should look like either a Porsche or high-end Cuisinart kitchen appliance, rather than some ugly, dated pieces of equipment. He fervently believed that Apple should not listen to Silicon Valley, but to high-end customers who aspired to buy Porsches.[8]

Second, Apple's retail stores are designed to be places in which customers can ask questions and get real answers. Unlike most companies that merely promise to give customer service (and then make it difficult for customers to actually reach a real person), Apple decided to ensure that every aspect of the retail store would be far away from anything that would remind customers of the bad experiences that they suffered from dealing with computers and high-tech gadgetry previously. Instore "Geniuses" will assist customers with setting up their iPods, iPads, iPhones and even help them with other non-Apple related products where they can. Even more stunning, Apple does not charge for any of these services except for those items out of warranty, and personnel have great leeway to drop those fees too.

A common theme that emerges is that Apple will always seek to cannibalize its own products quickly. Innovation is focused on the long-term, asking those questions that its rivals will not or cannot do so. Next generation iPhones are constantly under development, ready to replace models released a year previously. Even major changes to its operating systems are forward-looking, even if that means existing Apple users are compelled to upgrade their software to take advantage of the best features. Likewise, the company aims to accomplish what most other firms think is impossible. For example, it is believed that Apple is working on new types of products where the "future is built in."[9] This could mean computers that are "desk-free," or even three-dimensional

(3D) computing screens where holograms and voice recognition completely replace the need for keyboards and rigid screens.

Arenas

Where do we find Trendsetters? Trendsetters seek new markets opportunities and segments by tapping into some unmet need. Their value proposition revolves around a product or service offering that becomes a defining standard or benchmark for what customers feel they should receive for their purchases. Trendsetters can shape and markedly influence the evolution of the broader industry. They often become readily identified or even synonymous with a particular type of product or service in the customer's mind. But the Trendsetter's additional value does not always automatically mean a competitive advantage—customers must feel they receive a source of value they cannot get elsewhere. When Trendsetters can provide something very distinctive or even unique, this value proposition can prove extremely powerful.

In the food retailing industry, Whole Foods Market successfully tapped into the baby boomers' growing interest in health and well-being with organic foods complemented by superb customer service. Whole Foods Market is the United States' premier natural foods chain. It originated the concept of selling organic and health foods in a distinctive supermarket model encompassing some 350 plus stores. During Whole Foods' three decades-long expansion, organic and natural foods have become a huge segment of the overall grocery industry rather than the small market niche of old. With the company's wide assortment of distinctive foods, Whole Foods has been able to gain market share and customers even as major grocery store chains continue to lose ground to Wal-Mart Stores and other discount chains.

Whole Foods Market's success emanated from its early realization that many American customers wanted to live a lifestyle that supported better health and environmental sustainability. Founded by current CEO John Mackey, Whole Foods started in Austin, Texas, and its initial products included organic fruit and produce as well as hormone-free meat, grains, and chocolate. Many of Whole Foods' customers were willing to pay a markup of 20 per cent or more to attain a deep sense of personal satisfaction. This confirmed Mackey's original belief that people would aspire to purchase better products that offered them deeper fulfillment in their personal lives. Whole Foods also discovered that these customers were three times more likely than the general population to educate their friends and other people about the benefits of pursuing a healthier, more sustainable lifestyle.

Organic produce continues to make up approximately two-thirds of Whole Foods' revenues. As the company's core product, it attracts customers who often shop two to three times a week. This high frequency in turn encourages them to purchase other items as well. The average number of products purchased by a typical Whole Foods customer in any given transaction is much less than that of the major supermarket chains (meaning their check-out times are much shorter). However, their more frequent repeat purchase patterns mean they spend considerably more over any extended time period.[10]

Qualcomm, Inc. is one of the most important technology companies that make today's cell phones and smartphones work. Unlike Intel, Samsung, and other semiconductor giants, Qualcomm specializes in a narrow but critical technology space. Founded in 1985 by MIT alum Irwin Jacobs, Qualcomm today dominates the design of microchips that are found in phones made by Samsung, Motorola, HTC, LG, and Nokia. In 1990, Qualcomm designed a new technical standard known as CDMA (code-division multiplex architecture), which has steadily become the basis for much of the wireless phone technology used in the United States and elsewhere. Using technology that was first applied to managing transport fleets via satellite-tracking systems, Qualcomm realized that its CDMA technology could dramatically improve wireless phone communications since the airwaves were facing poor coverage and a shortage of capacity from overuse of the pre-existing technology. CDMA is a much more efficient digital transmission technology. It breaks (or "divides") a voice call or other signals across several different frequencies and then reassembles them at the other end. When telecom carriers use CDMA technology, they can dramatically increase the number of calls managed on their networks, since the calls do not interfere with one another. Ironically, the original idea to encode and divide a signal into multiple frequencies came from Hollywood actress Hedy Lamarr, who patented the concept in the United States in 1942. However, her concept was so new that the U.S. military did not adopt it to protect its communications during World War II.

Based on the significant royalty revenues that it earns from its CDMA technology, Qualcomm has broadened its focus to design all types of chips to enable greater mobility in digital devices. At the heart of Qualcomm's strategy is its continual push to expand the amount of wireless spectrum that next generation phones, online gaming devices, and tablets will consume. Its new Snapdragon microprocessor serves as the brains for a growing number of new Windows 8 and Android phones, which are made by a host of cell phone companies. Snapdragon offers much increased computing power and is also power-efficient, thus resulting in longer battery life. It is also highly versatile and can operate on a variety of advanced 4G/LTE networks. Arena-related issues for Trendsetters are summarized in Table 5.2.

Vehicles

Trendsetters rely heavily on internal product development and market research to better understand their customers' needs. Research, experimentation, advertising, and careful branding represent key pillars of Trendsetters' competitive advantage. But in many instances, the most important vehicle Trendsetters enjoy is a delighted customer who shares his or her experience with people who might become future customers. Capturing and building on demand momentum enables Trendsetters to carve out large market positions. That said, they are not

---

Table 5.2 Key Arena Issues for Trendsetters

- Identify and exploit an emerging or underserved need
- Focus on leading-edge offerings
- Start with a small niche; expand as opportunities avail

afraid of making selected acquisitions to complement their product portfolios. Acquisitions can rapidly boost a Trendsetter's market share while simultaneously gaining access to future technologies or leading brands that command awareness and customer loyalty.

L'Oréal is one of the best known cosmetics companies in the world. Based in France, L'Oréal was the brainchild of a French chemist who invented a new type of synthetic hair dye for women. The $26 billion company owns a stable of well-known brands, each a leader in its own category—Lancôme, Maybelline New York, Redken, Kiehl's, Helena Rubinstein, Soft Sheen, and Matrix. Historically, the company typically spends over 3 per cent of revenues on R&D, higher than the 2 per cent average for the cosmetics industry. A little known fact is that L'Oréal has applied for more nanotechnology patents than any other U.S. company.[11] Former CEO Sir Lindsay Owen-Jones cultivated a "cow and calf" culture, in which L'Oréal continuously invested in all types of R&D, even in those ventures that were not yet profitable. Owen-Jones noted that "a herd of cows exists only when it is producing calves and only a small proportion of the herd produces the milk."[12] This hidden side of L'Oréal masks an innovation machine that spans numerous scientific disciplines ranging from molecular biology to applied chemistry, nanotechnology, and even thin film substrates. L'Oréal's scientists are investigating and evaluating all types of research to improve its line of beauty products, and has even placed major bets on studying the underlying biochemical properties of immunology to promote self-healing in the skin. The company's research labs are distributed all around the world to take advantage of promising local talent, and to recognize that skin complexions, chemistries, and textures can vary significantly from one region to another. Despite its aggressive research posture, L'Oréal grew in the United States primarily through acquisition. With the exception of Lancôme, L'Oréal acquired all of the aforementioned brands during the 1980s and 1990s as it became more familiar with the demanding needs of the U.S. beauty market. The company likes to hire people with boundless energy and who act like entrepreneurs, seeking to be the first in what they do.[13]

Whole Foods has grown throughout the United States by locating its stores in mostly highly urban areas with high disposable incomes. CEO Mackey has expanded Whole Foods in a deliberate, methodical way to ensure that it is a welcome member of the neighborhood. The company designs the exterior of each store to match the surrounding real estate and the aesthetic sensitivities of its customers. To ensure that it can supply each of its stores, Whole Foods built its own distribution network, including bakeries that are located near a cluster of stores. It also carefully manages its supply chain with natural food vendors to ensure that they comply with Whole Foods' stringent quality requirements. Whole Foods even created its own line of private labels (e.g., Whole Foods, 360, Allegro, and Authentic Food Artisan) to ensure that customers can trust what they are buying. Whole Foods' private labels signify to consumers that they are buying products featuring the best ingredients that hold true to Whole Foods' mission of selling the freshest foods possible. To complement its fast internal growth, Whole Foods has selectively used acquisitions to bolster its market position. In 2007, it acquired Wild Oats, its arch-rival in many markets. In the New England region, Whole Foods even acquired its own fishery to ensure the timely delivery of its own catch.

Nike, Inc. is the world's largest supplier of athletic shoes and apparel and is a major producer of sporting equipment. Led by CEO Mark Parker, the company was founded as Blue Ribbon Sports by Phil Knight and track coach Bill Bowerman in 1962 before eventually becoming Nike in the 1970s. The company takes its name from the Greek goddess of victory. The $24.1 billion dollar giant (2012 revenues) deploys aggressive "celebrity marketing" and associates itself with college athletic teams, Olympic teams, and major professional sporting events throughout the world. Regardless of the type of shoe or apparel that Nike offers, the underlying vision behind the company is its relentless drive for high performance products. While Nike's aggressive marketing campaigns have brought us "The Swoosh" and the famous marketing slogan, "Just Do It," some of Nike's most powerful vehicles include its biomechanical R&D capabilities and funding of various community-based programs. Through internal development of new marketing programs and products, Nike constantly seeks to build brand awareness by offering leading-edge products but it also wants to inculcate a "sports mindset" in new markets that it enters.[14]

Nike possesses strong in-house R&D capabilities that have led to a number of major innovations. Known as the "Innovation Kitchen," Nike's think tank encourages its scientists to work closely with leading athletes and artists to think and design boldly—no holds barred. Products from the Kitchen include Nike Free, a training shoe, and Flywire, an ultra-thin thread based on the principles of building suspension bridges.[15] Nike's scientists work in such disciplines as biomechanics, exercise physiology, materials engineering, and industrial design. Nike even forms research committees and advisory boards composed of athletes, coaches, trainers, equipment managers, orthopedists, and podiatrists who work with Nike to review designs, materials, and new product concepts.

An early Nike innovation is its "Shox" technology, which features a special shoe cushion system that is especially designed for runners. (It can now be found in basketball shoes as well.) One of the most important developments that Nike has recently pioneered is its made-to-order shoe system known as "NikeID." This technical advance combines state-of-the-art design software and advanced manufacturing to offer customers a personalized shoe with all of their desired features at an affordable price. At the company's website (Nike.com), customers can envision what their personalized shoe will look like by clicking through 18 different color options, three sole choices, and two cushioning systems. There is also the capability to print your name or slogan on the shoe as well.

Nike has broadened the line of footwear, apparel, and even sporting equipment that it offers. In recent years, Nike has acquired Cole Haan, Converse, Hurley International, Bauer Italia S.p.A., and Official Starter. These important vehicles will extend Nike's deep knowledge of foot-wear into new market segments. Cole Haan enables Nike to sell upscale dress shoes, while Hurley designs and distributes a line of action sportswear for surfing and skateboarding. The Hurley brand also gives Nike better exposure to the youth lifestyle market. The primary vehicles used by Trendsetters to support their strategies is found in Table 5.3.

Table 5.3 Key Vehicle Issues for Trendsetters
• Internal development
• Encourage customers to share experiences with others
• Selective acquisitions to complement/expand products

Staging

By conceiving a new product or service concept, Trendsetters are constantly searching the environment for new market opportunities. Once Trendsetters identify a winning technology, product concept, or brand, they seek to leverage that asset to generate additional market opportunities. What begins as a concept that appeals to a narrow, limited audience steadily expands into adjacent, related markets, or derivative products that build on the original brand or design idea.

A well-respected brand can function as an umbrella for an expanding product lineup. Martha Stewart Living Omnimedia is a $221 million company (2011 figures) whose history and rise is inextricably tied to its eponymous founder. Ms. Stewart is perhaps best known as America's "domestic doyenne," who offers advice about how best to beautify a home, garden, and other interior décor. Her brand is based on achieving a style of "aesthetic perfection" in the home. In 1991, she launched *Martha Stewart Living* magazine in conjunction with Time, Inc. Shortly thereafter, she became famous for starring in *The Martha Stewart Show*, which offered all kinds of tips on better cleaning techniques as well as easy-to-do recipes and crafts. Many of these ideas also found their way into a line of cook and craft books found in department stores near the kitchenware aisles. After assuming full control of her company in 1997, Ms. Stewart then proceeded to leverage her brand by licensing her name to a broad range of merchandise, including bedding items, pet accessories, craft kits, Christmas decorations, and even a line of paints sold at The Home Depot.[16]

A core product idea can serve as the launch pad for derivative products that refine the original technology concept. Consider, for example, the sequence of steps that Apple has taken over the past decade to become the most desired provider of digital consumer electronics. Apple's brand equity and market value grew with each new product released to an eager market. In 2001, Apple introduced its first iPod, which enabled consumers to listen to music privately wherever they went. At the same time, Apple signed licensing deals with all of the major record label companies to ensure a steady legal stream of music that iPod listeners could purchase through Apple's iTunes stores. These licensing deals ensured that music companies were paid royalties and avoided legal complications for both Apple and its growing legions of customers. To reach out to wealthier consumers who wanted to make a fashion statement, Apple introduced the iPod Nano, but also created the iPod Shuffle that appealed to more budget-conscious customers who did not want to pay for the stylistic design and extra features of the Nano. In 2007, Apple introduced its first iPhone, which won rave reviews for its sleek design and incorporation of many new features, including the now ubiquitous touch-screen technology that removed the need for a cumbersome keyboard. After four subsequent iPhone upgrades (whose design added new features such as voice recognition and GPS positioning), Apple unveiled its most recent iPhone5 in September 2012. Of course, consumers' enjoyment of previous iPod and iPhone products generated the momentum that enabled Apple to launch its iPad tablets over the past few years with stunning success.[17]

When James Dyson first invented his air cyclone-based design vacuum cleaner in the early 1980s, he licensed the idea to a Japanese appliance company who built it in pink and sold it under the G-Force name in Japan. The machine was an immediate hit as customers viewed it as a fashion statement, rather than a cleaning device. Sales from the G-Force machines helped fund Dyson's investment in manufacturing and tooling so he could build his own machines in Britain. He also prefers to hire his own scientists and engineers, rather than rely on another firm to do the design work for him. Now, it is believed that Dyson commands over a thousand patents related to all types of technologies and proprietary designs for future appliances.[18] The Trendsetters' primary ways of staging their strategic activities are summarized in Table 5.4.

Table 5.4 Key Staging Issues for Trendsetters
• Build on early success to enter new markets • Develop umbrella branding • Create new product derivatives

Distinction

Distinction is what earns the Trendsetter customer loyalty over the long term. Of all the strategic pillars discussed, sustaining distinction is perhaps the most important for the Trendsetter's strategy as it enables the Trendsetter to grow faster and to forestall imitation from rivals. Highly distinctive products and unique customer service allow Trendsetters to set higher prices as well. Trendsetters thrive when they offer customers a value proposition that is highly specialized, leading-edge, and/or offers a high degree of personalization and a fast response to their needs. Although the Trendsetter's offerings attract customers, execution is the foundation of distinction. Whether it is innovating new products or delivering the best service, distinction springs forth from organization design—the part of the business that customers rarely see.

Today's films are full of special effects that dazzle the mind. Yet, most films produced by Hollywood actually lose money! However, the animated films produced by Pixar Animation Studios, now a unit of The Walt Disney Company, made cinematic history in 1995 with its smash-hit *Toy Story*. Ever since, Pixar has led the way in creating thirteen entertaining animation films (including sequels to *Toy Story*, *Finding Nemo*, *The Incredibles*, *A Bug's Life*, *Cars*, and *Monsters*) using some of the most sophisticated computer and graphics technology available behind the scenes. Amazingly, the company has generated over $7 billion in revenues, with the highest gross average revenue per film in the industry. To this date, Pixar has earned over 26 Academy Awards and seven Golden Globes. What is the source of Pixar's distinction? It is the way that it fosters internal collaboration among its writers, directors, animators, and technical staff who work together on project after project. This methodical process enables Pixar to quickly transfer the learning and experiences garnered from making one film to other ongoing film projects. Unlike most Hollywood studios, which typically hire freelance writers and technical personnel to work on a film and then dispense with their services, Pixar creates an organizational memory of how it can create better films requiring less time in the future. There is a uniquely strong sense of mutual trust among Pixar's creative talent departments that enables them, by using its own staff, to communicate and critique each other's efforts in ways that other Hollywood studios cannot emulate because of the latter's use of external contractors.[19]

Most Trendsetters achieve distinction by balancing the underlying organizational tension between high autonomy and high conformity to demanding standards. In most organizations, senior management tends to regard autonomy and conformity as a tradeoff. To achieve system-wide conformity, the organization becomes overly centralized, thus stifling the incentive and ability of employees and on-site managers to think on their own, to respond quickly, and to do whatever it takes to help customers. People fear that they will be punished if they act out of accordance with internal procedures. On the other hand, in organizations that overplay the benefits of high autonomy, product and service consistency may be uneven, since guidelines and standards are not rigidly enforced or monitored. The Ritz-Carlton has achieved distinction through an organization design that promotes both. Even though, as noted above, the Ritz gathers data on every possible activity that occurs in each hotel, management and employee training remain central to how well they embody The Ritz-Carlton's culture of high-touch customer service. Throughout the system, all employees are taught an acronym known as "Mr. Biv." Mr. Biv stands for Mistakes, Reworks, Breakdowns, Inefficiencies, and Variations in work practices. Managers and employees are evaluated according to how well they implement Mr. Biv in every task they perform. This ensures that the customer receives the most responsive level of service and simultaneously unleashes employees to do their jobs in the best possible way.[20] Following the logic of Mr. Biv encourages employees to live and breathe The Ritz-Carlton Credo: "... fulfills even the unexpressed wishes and needs of our guests."[21] The critical sources of distinction for Trendsetters are found in Table 5.5.

Table 5.5 Ways to Achieve Distinction for Trendsetters
• Earn lifelong customer loyalty
• Create internal processes that focus on customer service
• Anticipate future customer needs by thinking from their perspective
• Encourage employees to pursue the highest standards of performance
• Promote fast product innovation

Economic Logic

Price inelasticity and customer loyalty represent the underpinnings of Trendsetters' economic logic. Price inelasticity means that customers are willing to pay more for a Trendsetter's product, even when there are similar competitive offerings available. Trendsetters hope to capture an economic nirvana of two worlds: high prices and frequent customer repeat purchases. In reality, pricing is only part of the value equation. Customers must feel that they are getting significantly more value from the Trendsetter (higher price but considerably more benefit) than from a rival that offers a lower price (but with much less benefit or customer intimacy).

People freely shop at Whole Foods because it offers them not only high-quality food with the freshest ingredients, but also a deep personal satisfaction that they bought something far from ordinary. Whole Foods' values of healthy living and environmental sustainability are much more in sync with its customers' emotional needs. This personal satisfaction is part of the total value that the customer receives. Although customers can now easily purchase organic, preservative-free foods at established supermarket chains, they will probably not obtain the same degree of emotional satisfaction. Prices at Whole Foods stores are often much higher than those in neighboring supermarket chains offering standardized products. Some Wall Street analysts have been known to joke that Whole Foods should change its name to "Whole Paycheck" to reflect the high dollar amount spent by customers. Likewise, zealous Apple customers have no hesitation standing in long lines (sometimes overnight, to keep their place) to be among the first people to purchase the latest Apple gadget (iPhone, iPad tablet) for several hundreds dollars more than a similar but older, less sexy, or less versatile model from Amazon, Motorola, Nokia, or HTC. After waiting all night, being among the first to leave a store holding a sleek, fashionable Apple-labeled gadget satisfies the customer's emotional needs in a major way.

Trendsetters can benefit from possessing proprietary technologies or standards that lock in customers to their offerings. Apple benefits significantly from the fact that it owns several proprietary technologies that make it difficult for customers to switch to other vendors. Apple has closely tied the music-listening features of its iPod and iPhone gadgets to its iTunes store, which sells tens of thousands of music files. The iTunes store has also become an outlet for an ever-expanding universe of "apps" that work seamlessly with the iPhone and iPad tablet. Customers can easily use both devices to search for whatever "app" they want and purchase it immediately. Some observers note that the iTunes store, combined with the iPad, create the perfect platform for offering potential video streaming services that could challenge today's television broadcasting. Apple also captures significant economic benefits by keeping its iPhone operating system proprietary. This insulates the iPhone from direct pricing pressures and encroachment by Google's Android system. Although Google licenses its system to numerous handset device makers, Apple keeps its system available only for Apple appliances, which adds further to the halo and special appeal of its products.

Dyson's desire to do its own design work in-house enables the company to enshroud future product plans in a high degree of secrecy. It also prevents competitors from directly emulating his proprietary ideas, thus undercutting the aura and high prices the firm can charge. The company hires its own engineers to work on futuristic, leading-edge product ideas, protecting them from prying eyes. Dyson acknowledges that when he introduced his "cyclone" technology in earlier years, he felt that large appliance makers that licensed his design may have taken advantage of him. Years of litigation almost cost Dyson his company as he fought to protect his unique design from being copied by lower-cost manufacturers.

Strategic Discipline: Customer Intimacy

The kernel of competitive advantage for Trendsetters is an intimacy which allows them to discover, learn, improve, and offer new products and services directly targeted at their customers. This emphasis on close, personal interaction with the customer offers the Trendsetter numerous vantage points to acquire insights that may become the basis for future product and service opportunities. As we have seen from The Ritz-Carlton example, the highest form of customer intimacy occurs when the company is able to think like its customer.

Every organization should be able to deliver a quality product or service and stand behind it. This is the minimum baseline of any business. Customer intimacy is vastly different. Intimacy transcends meeting needs; it is the provision of anticipatory, proactive value to the customer. "Anticipatory" means truly understanding the customer at the deepest level—even to the point of understanding his or her emotional and subconscious needs where possible. "Proactive" means providing them before the customer is even aware of what he or she desires. An excellent insight by Micah Solomon asserts that anticipatory customer service actually means that there is little distinction between "product" and "service"—the two come together as a source of value that addresses economic and emotional needs simultaneously. Achieving maximum customer satisfaction means building a high level of emotional connection into the product itself if possible.[22]

Previous research by Greer and Lei argue that the most customer-intimate, "empathetic" organizations enable the customer to shape the buying experience in their own personal context. This means deeply understanding any given customer's functional/performance requirements, making sense and articulating the surrounding emotional factors that may greatly impact how the customer will ultimately regard and use the product or solution that is offered. The emotional context of how the product is developed, offered, and used is as important, if not more so, than the product's performance. To develop this sense-making capability, intimate, "empathetic" organizations must be able to help customers discover and learn for themselves how they can make the product or solution a part of their own special emotional experience.

Deep customer intimacy occurs when organizations believe that they are contributing something meaningful to their customers' lives; ideally, their products evoke such emotional responses as joy, pride, achievement, and personal satisfaction.[23] This is a big part of the competitive advantage that Apple, The Ritz-Carlton, and Sewell Automotive enjoy.

Attaining customer intimacy requires the organization to compete along these dimensions:

1. creating experiences;
2. fast cycle innovation;
3. customer empowerment;
4. a service process mindset.

Creating Experiences

Trendsetters build the most enduring competitive advantages when they are able to create memorable experiences for their customers. Carl Sewell is famous for his commentary: "If the customer asks, the answer is always yes."[24] Trendsetters should listen on many levels. There is what the customer tells you verbally, and there are signals that he/she may be giving off that send a very different message. As noted above, employees at The Ritz-Carlton and rival Four Seasons are intensively trained to sense and read a customer's body language and subtle signals. This skill encourages them to anticipate what customers want.

Simply getting close to customers does not create an understanding of their deeper emotional needs, since businesses have their own biases and blinders about what customers should expect. This explains why market research studies in themselves provide only the most superficial information. No matter how much the large supermarket chains spend on their organic food initiatives, they cannot easily connect with their customers because the values of the two parties are out of alignment. Likewise, merely inquiring about customers' needs provides only partial information because customers are unlikely to verbalize a description of a new product or request one when they cannot imagine or spell out their vision of an ideal product, as Apple's competitors have learned to their chagrin. Sometimes, customers are unlikely to request a new improved service when they are conditioned to accept deficiencies as the normal state of affairs, as Richard Branson discovered in his numerous business start-ups organized around creating a fun experience (e.g., Virgin Music, Virgin Mobile, and Virgin Atlantic).

As legions of American baby boomers gravitate to buying its legendary motorcycles, Harley-Davidson has fostered an ongoing strategy to communicate with its customers at its retail outlets, at special promotions, and at its heralded open-road tours. The company's Harley Owners Group (HOG), which was founded to enhance communications with customers, is now the world's largest motorcycle club. The company's close interactions with its customers enable managers to understand and capture the personal emotions and experiences they associate with Harley-Davidson's machines. Harley's engineers try to design each generation of motorcycles to capture the unique American spirit of its users. Buying a Harley is buying an experience. Now, entire families— often spanning two or three generations—are committed to the company's products, programs, and other marketing initiatives. There is even an extensive line of branded Harley-Davidson fashions, not to mention a special line of Harley-Davidson trucks built by Ford, for the truly committed customer. In addition, the company offers an extensive line of accessory products that allows customers to customize their motorcycles and experience the Harley-Davidson story.[25] What other company do you know that has its logo tattooed on its customers' bodies?

Fast Cycle Innovation

Streamlining product development and slicing time-to-market are the lifeblood of Trendsetters' innovation strategy. Product innovation should accomplish two key objectives: first, avoid commoditization from rivals introducing a similar lower-priced offering; second, stay ahead of customers' evolving needs. Trendsetters sustain their competitive advantage when they conceive and "futurize" next-generation products and technologies that far exceed customers' expectations. Delighting customers with unexpected product and service features keeps the Trendsetters' offerings fresh and forestalls competitive imitation. The Trendsetters' core product concept offers the potential to expand into new arenas, but it must continue to champion the customer in its product development process.

One phenomenon impacting all industries is the following: the pace of innovation accelerates as one moves from the lab to the customer.[26] For example, it is not uncommon for internal R&D programs to think in terms of months and years to conceive, engineer, and test a prototype before a single product is introduced to the marketplace. Manufacturing the product requires investment, but changing the tooling, dyes, and assembly equipment typically needs a few weeks. When the business comes in direct contact with customers (whether in person or through any channel), it must respond to their needs instantly in order to provide satisfaction. Therefore, successfully competing on time means injecting the customers' sense of urgency and the need for fast response into all aspects of the business's activities. Top-notch Trendsetters like Andrews Distributing realize that by thinking like a customer, they can design state-of-the-art processes from the ground up that dramatically reduce or even eliminate time lags and wastes in their value-creating system.

Nike's biomechanical labs incorporate hundreds of sensors in different types of running tracks (e.g., artificial turf, grass, concrete, pavement, and sand) to measure the pressure, torque, and twisting effects on athletic shoes under development. This ultra-modern facility allows Nike's scientists to conceive and test a variety of different advanced proprietary materials, such as gels, silicates, and plastic composites. Successful testing of these new materials often takes years to ensure their safety and product applicability. However, to accelerate time-to-market, Nike asks athletes—for instance, Kobe Bryant—to work directly with its engineers and product specialists to see which candidate shoe materials and configurations work best. Nike collaborates with sports-people to test every dimension of performance. Because aesthetics also matter greatly to top performers, Nike imbues a relevant artistic style to each shoe model. Close product testing and idea-sharing between Nike's staff and star athletes help Nike to stay fresh and a powerful brand in consumers' minds. As a big side benefit, Nike's research contributes major insight to biomedical research as well. For example, the stress and strain that muscles and bones confront in highly athletic activities can provide valuable insight into what kinds of next-generation synthetic bone materials or prosthetics can be used to speed up the healing of fractures and other injuries. This valuable information captured in Nike's research can prove exceptionally useful to the medical profession.

Customer Empowerment

Attaining customer intimacy is really an application of Maslow's hierarchy of needs:[27] once a customer's basic economic needs are met, he or she will strive to fulfill other needs in order to achieve higher personal satisfaction. Most of these needs revolve around making customers feel better about themselves. Ultimately, the highest human need is self-actualization or the need to accomplish what a person wants to do. Trendsetters win and retain customers when they enable customers to feel empowered. One growing trend in many industries is the rise of co-creation, whereby customers co-design the products they want with their providers. Co-creation means that the firm and the customer jointly develop new product ideas. Trendsetters that foster ongoing customer involvement in developing product ideas may in turn help customers receive satisfaction of emotional or psychic needs, thus further strengthening customer loyalty. Collaborating with customers provides a means for enhancing faster innovation, but firms must first have a comprehensive understanding of how its offerings fit the customer's total needs. Increasingly, collaborative innovation with customers is becoming a major component of many organizations' product and service developmental efforts.

For example, product development at Apple is less about technology than imagining how customers want to use technology to achieve satisfaction in their personal lives. Delivering superior performance chips, software, LCD screens, and hard drives is not the focus of Apple's R&D; rather they are instruments that facilitate faster and more enjoyable customer experiences for Apple's users. Apple's relentless efforts to incorporate voice recognition, GPS features, ever thinner and smaller gadgets, and instant connectivity with automobile docking devices are designed to uncomplicate the user's experience. Technology by itself is nothing more than a tool that helps unleash new ways to understand and satisfy the customer.

The Container Store views itself as a lifestyle retailer because the store's products help people organize their lives as well as their homes. As one Container Store representative says, "time is what we sell." The nature of this more intimate and emotional relationship of the intimate "empathetic" organization is revealed in The Container Store's principle of the man in the desert, as described by a manager to a *Fortune* magazine reporter working in one of the stores for a week:

> The man in the desert is the story of a man crawling through the desert gasping for water. He comes to an oasis, where a regular retailer gives him water. Well, he thinks, 'Great.' But when he comes to the Container Store, we say, 'Here's some water, and how about some food? I see that you have a wedding ring on. Can we call your family and let them know you're here?' This applies to customers: It doesn't do any good to hand them a glass of water without the food. You're cheating the customer if you're not offering them the opportunity to buy more.

When The Container Store works with a customer to provide customized solutions to a problem of disorganized closets or drawers, a messy teenager's room, or the garage of a husband who has a penchant for unfinished projects, it has a more intimate relationship than many service interactions or retail transactions. The customer's relationship with family members may be revealed as he or she and the employee work to jointly solve the problem. For example, a customer may say, "My daughter just throws her clothes on the floor in her room like she expects me to pick up after her." This close relationship may be captured in a humorous comment as The Container Store chairman and co-founder, Garrett Boone, says, coming to The Container Store is "cheaper than [going to] a shrink."[28]

A Service Process Mindset

Thinking like a customer means designing each step of the business in the way the customer would want it done. Why does the customer come to us? What do we offer of value? What are his/her emotional as well as economic needs? These are the starting questions that every business should ask itself. And yet, all too often, most organizations look at customer service from an internal perspective, or even worse, as an afterthought. Paradoxically, some organizations will invest heavily in new technologies to minimize personal customer contact: notice the proliferation of "telephone trees" in most automated customer service departments that force a customer to jump through numerous hoops, only to wait a long time before anyone even picks up. Errors, unsatisfied customers, poorly trained employees, and slow response times destroy brand equity. Most businesses forget that the most important intelligence gathering tool they possess is their own eyes and ears, rather than complex market research data that yield little meaningful insight.

Trendsetters that tightly link their internal processes to their customer's emotional and economic needs are extremely well-positioned to capture his/her loyalty. Creating an anticipatory service logic and mindset throughout the firm, however, requires designing a customer-centric process that often upends conventional thinking about how to organize a business' activities. These processes should be robust (capable of handling unexpected customer requests), flexible (to handle unforeseen or sudden needs), and scalable (expandable so that customers do not have to wait to gain personal attention). "Systems, not smiles," according to Carl Sewell, is the key to delivering an excellent product or service each and every time. When there are only smiles and no systems, the smiles eventually disappear when the customer finds that his or her needs were not met.

Nordstrom's "Personal Book" embodies a powerful combination of technology with human insight and interaction to create fervently loyal customers. A record of each customer's preferences, previous purchase history, and list of possible items he or she may wish to purchase in the future, the Personal Book enables a Nordstrom salesperson to quickly offer personalized service and to engage in a relevant conversation with the customer. This information is stored electronically and stays with the company even when that salesperson leaves. Employees are encouraged to use the Personal Book to anticipate what their customers may want. For example, if Nordstrom salespeople knew the shoe size or tie color that a customer desired, they could then set aside a few pairs of shoes or a small sample of ties and inform the customer of their availability. However, the customer does not see the other side of Nordstrom's process: the shoe stocking area is sorted by color, size, heel size, and designer label so that the salesperson can readily find the customer's possible choices with little time lost. When a customer makes a purchase, the Nordstrom salesperson sends a handwritten thank you note to the customer.[29]

Strategic Dangers for Trendsetters

Trendsetters create significant competitive advantage through their product and service innovations. They generate deep loyalty among their customers but are vulnerable to some important dangers:

1. the quicksand of brand dilution;
2. bloated cost structures;
3. losing sight of the customer.

The strategic vulnerabilities of Trendsetters are presented in Table 5.6.

The Quicksand of Brand Dilution

Trendsetters run the potential risk of strategic overextension in several ways. First, they can produce too many different variations of their core product offering, thus confusing the customer. Second, they may also attempt to use their brand on too many products, resulting in customers asking themselves "What is this brand really about?" In both situations, the Trendsetter can overextend itself to such an extent that it begins to

---

Table 5.6 Perils of Trendsetters

- Overexpansion leads to potential brand dilution
- Costs can rise to dangerous levels
- Success can result in losing sight of the customer

sink into an economic quicksand where the economic logic of its business dies out. When Trendsetters attempt to leverage their brand equity into new markets that share little commonality with their core business, they can face significant dilution of their brand equity.

Consider the numerous difficulties confronting Starbucks over the past several years. CEO Howard Schulz realized that its spectacular rise from a Seattle-based coffee house offering distinctive and high-priced blends of coffees to a global powerhouse in coffees, cold beverages, music, and even movies overextended the firm. Even though Starbucks customers enjoyed the company's brews, experimentation with cooked breakfasts and pre-packaged sandwiches diluted the distinctive coffee-based aromas that people had become accustomed to associating with a Starbucks outlet. The aroma issue was compounded by the efficiency-driven move into using pre-ground coffee, rather than grinding it on-site—a misstep Starbucks has since reversed. In addition, Starbucks' ventures into music and then movies steadily eroded the firm's brand equity, as customers began to wonder what the company really stood for. To compound matters, Starbucks reached its culminating point of expansion just as the global economy went into a tailspin in 2008. High-priced lattes and brews became a luxury, compelling customers to retreat from purchasing high-priced Starbucks coffee for lower-priced offerings from McDonald's and Dunkin' Donuts. Consequently, CEO Schulz announced that the company would be closing a number of stores in the United States as it seeks to reboot its business and refocus on training its barristas to recapture Starbucks' original mission of providing great coffee in a comfortable "Third Living Room" environment.

Martha Stewart Living Omnimedia is facing a major test of its strategy as the company suffers from excessive branding of its namesake on a huge range of products; its value has been diluted and what it really stands for lost. In addition, the brand is not catching on with younger urban audiences, who are less likely to cook, clean, and do other household chores for themselves. Hammered by a major downturn in advertising spending for its line of Martha Stewart magazines, the company is in the midst of major litigation, as it signed a long-term cross-marketing arrangement with J.C. Penney in exchange for a much-needed cash infusion. This new relationship is not without complications, however, as a current relationship with Macy's has begun to sour. Macy's claims that by joining forces with J.C. Penney, Martha Stewart is undercutting the ability to design and sell products through Macy's stores. In addition, Martha Stewart's television show ratings are dropping, as newer reality cooking shows begin to grab large audiences. Ms. Stewart herself has commented that one of her most urgent priorities is to fix the disconnect between her persona and the company's performance. To reverse the company's misfortunes, the company announced that it would discontinue publishing two of its magazines and lay off roughly 12 per cent of its staff. Both magazines will be offered periodically as digital supplements to the flagship *Martha Stewart Living* magazine.[30]

In the 1990s, both Krispy Kreme and Tiffany & Co. faced a similar strategic situation when both companies started to offer products that diluted brand strengths. In the case of Krispy Kreme, this baker of highly distinctive doughnuts has long been the Trendsetter for this food category. Throughout its early history, people would stand in line, sometimes for up to an hour, to wait for their turn to purchase Krispy Kreme doughnuts from a retail shop that featured a unique look. The mystique surrounding Krispy Kreme doughnuts grew throughout the 1990s as word spread about its remarkable taste and consistency. The company also deliberately kept the number of its nationwide retail locations small to avoid saturating the market. However, by the beginning of the last decade, Krispy Kreme began to expand rapidly. It also began selling its highly-cherished doughnuts through gas stations, Target stores in the United States, Tesco supermarkets in the United Kingdom, and elsewhere. As the aura surrounding Krispy Kreme's doughnuts faded, so did the company's fortunes.

Tiffany & Co. is considered one of the blue-chip names of luxury fashion items. Best known for its distinctive blue boxes that often signified a gift designed to enchant and delight, Tiffany's believed that it needed to attract a younger audience, since the vast majority of its sales came from people well into their fifties. Realizing that a younger market would not have the same disposable income as its traditional core customer, Tiffany's began selling lower grades of less expensive silver jewelry at much lower price points. Although this move brought in additional foot traffic, many young customers felt overawed by Tiffany's more formal style, both in terms of its jewelry designs and the delivery of customer service. Names of exclusive, famous designers such as Paloma Picasso and Elsa Peretti did not resonate with younger customers. As a result, Tiffany's has scaled back its promotional efforts geared to that segment. However, Tiffany's currently still runs the risk of brand dilution. It has steadily expanded the number of stores throughout the United States by moving away from ultra-wealthy zip codes to smaller-sized cities. This move also runs the risk that Tiffany's may lose its exclusivity and its cherished brand.

Bloated Cost Structures

Trendsetters run a major risk of inflating their cost structures as they spend large sums on expanding their core product concepts and innovating future offerings. Many Trendsetters invest heavily in R&D efforts that often take an extended time to pay off. More important, Trendsetters often encounter redundant efforts and duplication of functional activities as their organizational structures emphasize a more decentralized management approach.

Dallas-based restaurant firm Brinker International has long exhibited the strategic hallmarks of a Trendsetter with its wildly popular Chili's restaurant chain. The company has delivered steady growth over two decades and began undertaking a series of acquisitions in the mid-1990s. Brinker's acquisition of The Corner Bakery in the late 1990s was originally predicated on building important business synergies because it had operations—for example, Chili's, On-The-Border, and Romano's Macaroni Grill—that could share key functions, such as baking. Brinker was able to replicate its supply chain, logistics systems, hiring practices, market research capabilities, and other competencies to service this new arena. However, over the past ten years, Brinker sold off many of its acquisitions as the desired synergies failed to materialize. Coordination among the units became difficult to manage and slowed the company down. In 2007, Brinker announced that it would sell almost 80 per cent of its Romano's Macaroni Grill unit to renew its focus on its core Chili's restaurants and recently sold The Corner Bakery. Now, with over 1,300 Chili's units, the company is studying new ways to improve the efficiency of its service operations. It discovered that employees spend too much time performing individual tasks without coordinating their work with each other. Investment in new ovens that combine both the skillet and the smoker will help reduce the duplication of work in the kitchen and help employees better focus on the customer.[31]

Losing Sight of the Customer

Perhaps the greatest mortal danger to Trendsetters is losing their customers' trust and loyalty. With the expansion that accompanies continued success, Trendsetters can fall into the trap of becoming more focused on internal reporting requirements and procedures, rather than staying close and understanding the customer. Expansion represents a double-edged sword. Trendsetters yearn to set the industry standard for performance and customer satisfaction, but once they have discovered a successful core product or service concept, they run the risk of letting success become an accepted status quo. Common symptoms of this weakness include a Not-Invented-Here (NIH) syndrome, a riveting focus on financial metrics of performance at the cost of customer satisfaction, and a belief that rivals will be unable to decipher the secrets of the Trendsetter's success. This danger is especially troubling when the Trendsetters inevitably encounter a slower growth in their industry, customers become increasingly price-sensitive, and rivals become more adept at imitating the Trendsetter's offerings.

Consider the danger that Nordstrom narrowly avoided in the early 2000s. In the midst of a major nationwide expansion that brought the upscale shoe and fashion retailer to numerous U.S. cities, Nordstrom was slow to adapt to some major changes occurring within the industry. First, Nordstrom's emphasis on highly personalized customer service meant that stores were managed in a highly decentralized manner. Shared purchasing of shoes, clothing and other merchandise among Nordstrom stores was an alien concept to store managers and buyers, who typically sought out the merchandise most likely to sell in a given region. Also, Nordstrom employees often placed extra orders for merchandise that ultimately did not sell, since they wanted a wide product availability to satisfy their customers' needs in the Personal Book discussed above. Second, Nordstrom was also late in implementing modern "perpetual inventory replenishment" systems. These systems track every purchase through bar codes and can give store managers, regional managers, and corporate headquarters a day-to-day breakdown of what sells in which store. Without such inventory systems, Nordstrom was essentially flying blind and periodically found itself caught with merchandise imbalances that necessitated occasional deep discounting. Finally, Nordstrom tried to market itself to a much younger customer base, as Tiffany & Co. attempted to do so in jewelry. Instead of featuring instrumental music played live on a piano in the middle of the store, Nordstrom introduced more avant-garde music that alienated many of its longstanding core customers. Fortunately, within a few years of recognizing the damaging effects on its brand, Nordstrom management returned the company to its core business of offering highly sought after shoes and fashions to well-heeled customers. The company eventually installed a state-of-the-art inventory tracking system that helped lower its costs and limit the need for deep discounts of unsold items.

MASTERING THE ESSENTIALS OF A TRENDSETTER

Mastering the essentials of a trendsetter involves:

- developing a deep, empathetic understanding of the customer;
- innovating new products and services that anticipate what the customer wants;
- ensuring that the firm's offerings and brand never become stale;
- becoming the industry leader or standard for customer-driven performance;

and avoiding the following:

- entering too many new markets so that brand dilution ensues;
- neglecting costs so that pricing becomes uncompetitive;
- failing to listen to, and to anticipate, future customer needs.

Notes

1 Carl Sewell, *Customers for Life*, Crown Business, New York, 2002.
2 Emily Ross and Angus Holland, "Dyson: Suck It and See," *100 Great Businesses and the Minds Behind Them*, Sourcebooks, Naperville, IL, 2006, pp. 40–44.
3 A more extensive study of The Container Store's strategy and the broader notion of customer involvement in co-designing solutions can be found in D. Lei and C. R. Greer, "The Empathetic Organization," *Organizational Dynamics*, Volume 32, Number 2, 2003, pp. 162–164.
4 See "PetSmart Thrives Treating Owners Like Parents," *Wall Street Journal*, September 12, 2012, p. B7.
5 See J. Robinson, "How The Ritz-Carlton Manages the Mystique," *Gallup Management Journal*, December 11, 2008.
6 An outstanding discussion of Nintendo's strategy to create "customer momentum" to delight customers is Jean-Claude Larreché's *The Momentum Effect*, Wharton School Publishing, Upper Saddle River, NJ, 2008.
7 For example, see Ken Segall, *Insanely Simple: The Obsession That Drives Apple's Success*, Penguin, New York, 2012. Also see Carmine Gallo, *The Apple Experience: Secrets to Building Insanely Great Customer Loyalty*, McGraw-Hill, New York, 2012.
8 See "Apple Nation," *Fast Company*, July–August 2010, pp. 68–76, 112.
9 Ibid.
10 J. R. Wells and T. Haglock, "Whole Foods Market, Inc.," Harvard Business School Case 9–705-476.
11 See "Picking the Winners," *Forbes*, August 8, 2011, p. 78.
12 Emily Ross and Angus Holland, "L'Oréal: Foster a 'cow and calf' culture," *100 Great Businesses and the Minds Behind Them*, Sourcebooks, Naperville, IL, 2006, pp. 258–260.
13 G. Jones, D. Kiron, V. Dessain, and A. Sjoman, "L'Oréal and the Globalization of American Beauty," Harvard Business School Case 9–805-086.
14 See "Nike Builds Sports Mindset in Market," *Wall Street Journal*, October 12, 2011, p. B7.
15 See "Artist. Athlete. CEO." *Fast Company*, September 2010, pp. 66–74, 110.
16 See "Domestic Discord: Martha Stewart Seeks Perfect Touch For Her Empire," *Wall Street Journal*, August 25–26, 2012, pp. A1, A10.
17 See "For Dominating the Business Landscape in 101 Ways," *Fast Company*, March 2011, pp. 68–76.
18 Emily Ross and Angus Holland, "Dyson: Suck It and See," *100 Great Businesses and the Minds Behind Them*, Sourcebooks, Naperville, IL, 2006, pp. 40–44.
19 See "Animating a Blockbuster: Inside Pixar's Creative Magic," *Wired*, June 2010, pp. 140–145.
20 Micah Solomon, *High-Tech, High-Touch Customer Service*, AMACON, New York, 2012, p. 105.
21 See Micah Solomon, *High-Tech, High-Touch Customer Service*, AMACON, New York, 2012, pp. 49–50.
22 Micah Solomon, *High-Tech, High-Touch Customer Service*, AMACON, New York, 2012, p. 62.
23 "The Empathetic Organization," *Organizational Dynamics*, Volume 32, Number 2, 2003.
24 Carl Sewell, *Customers for Life*, Crown Business, New York, 2002, pp. 12–15.

25 "The Empathetic Organization," *Organizational Dynamics*, Volume 32, Number 2, 2003. Also see R. Teerlink, "Harley's Leadership U-Turn," *Harvard Business Review*, July–August 2000, pp. 43–48.

26 An excellent overview of this premise is found in Charles Fine, *Clockspeed*, Perseus Book Group, New York, 1998.

27 Maslow's hierarchy of needs states that people will first satisfy their physical needs for food, shelter and security. After that, people will strive for relationships, emotional fulfillment, and ultimately "self-actualization," which means they discover the true meaning of what their life is about.

28 "The Empathetic Organization," *Organizational Dynamics*, Volume 32, Number 2, 2003. Also, "My Job at the Container Store," *Fortune*, January 10, 2000, pp. 74–78, and Martin Delahoussaye, "In Person: Melissa Reiff, Vice President Sales and Marketing, The Container Store," *Training*, Vol. 38, No. 4, 2001, pp. 36–37.

29 R. Lal and A. Han, "Nordstrom: The Turnaround," Harvard Business School Case 9–505-051.

30 See "Martha Stewart Pares Magazines," *Wall Street Journal*, November 2, 2012, p. B6.

31 See "Chili's Feels Heat to Pare Costs," *Wall Street Journal*, January 28, 2011, p. B8.

6

CONSOLIDATORS

Every industry, whether it is fast food, consumer electronics, video games, or travel, confronts the reality that growth ultimately slows down. The hallmarks of industry maturity include the recognition that:

- products are standardized;
- markets are saturated;
- customers are smarter;
- organizations slow down.

Maturity often means that competition is fast approaching a zero-sum game, where one firm's economic gain comes at the expense of another. As total industry revenue grows slowly—or even contracts—competitors can find themselves saddled with fixed costs that work against profitability. To the extent that customers cannot distinguish among competing firms' offerings, price becomes the primary point of differentiation as value propositions become increasingly similar. As a result, customers migrate to whichever business can provide them the best deal at that moment.

Over the past decade or so, the pressure to earn profitable returns has transformed the U.S. economic landscape of a vast array of industries. Massive operational investments, multi-billion dollar acquisitions and complex strategic alliances have produced enormously powerful firms in their respective markets. For example, Aetna, Cigna and WellPoint (managed health-care plans); UnitedContinental Holdings and Delta (airlines); UPS and FedEx (shipping and logistics); Safeway and Kroger (grocery retailing); Wal-Mart and Target (discount retailers); ConAgra, H. J. Heinz and General Mills (food processing); Amazon (Internet retailing); AT&T and Verizon (telecommunications); and Micron Technology (memory chips) are well-known firms whose industries have faced maturity. All of these industries currently have to contend with slowing growth, price wars, high fixed costs, and the growing ease with which customers can switch from one provider or vendor to another. Even industries once considered the breeding ground of high-profile innovators and legendary brand names are now caught in the vise of maturity pressures. These include older cell phones, consumer electronics, wireless companies, and even Internet-service providers.

Businesses that once led industries or shaped the customer's mindset for exceptional product quality or customer service are not immune from industry maturity. In a paradoxical way, maturity is the byproduct of long-term industry success stretching over earlier time periods. Industries become mature precisely because businesses have become so successful in expanding, fine-tuning and refining what they offer to their customers. Customers, in turn, begin to view today's leading-edge offerings as business as usual tomorrow. As industry growth rates slow down and innovations become more incremental, a new strategic imperative kicks in: consolidation. The major strategic and organizational hallmarks of the Consolidator are captured in Figure 6.1.

Attempting to Recapture the Industry Initiative

To navigate and survive the transition to industry maturity, consolidators must pursue:

1. reduced competition;
2. economies of scale;
3. greater bargaining power over suppliers and buyers;

4. the primacy of cost-efficient operations in guiding investment decisions.[1]

Reducing Competition

A decrease in the number of providers in a given market will lead to more stable pricing, lower customer acquisition costs, and a further standardization of product offerings' features. When there are too many providers in one particular market, pricing remains unstable and customers can freely switch from one firm to another. To reduce industry-wide competition, businesses can either merge and acquire their rivals or divest themselves of market positions that are too costly to sustain. Consider, for example, how brutal industry conditions have reshaped the U.S. airline and telecommunications businesses in the past ten years. Airline businesses are completing another wave of mergers with the creation of a much larger Delta Airlines;

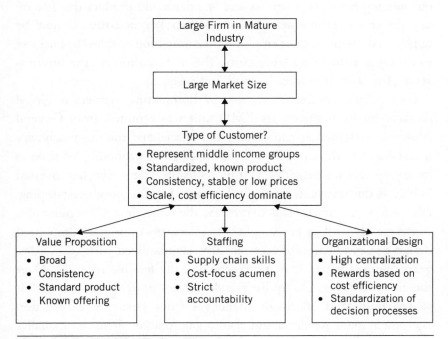

Figure 6.1 The Foundation of a Consolidator.

UnitedContinental (the product itself of several restructurings during the 1980s and 1990s) and even Southwest Airlines' acquisition of rival AirTrans. In the telecommunications industry, a seemingly endless series of mergers occurred just this past decade—Verizon (Bell Atlantic and GTE), AT&T (Southwestern Bell, Cingular Wireless), T-Mobile (a collection of regional wireless companies once known as VoiceStream Wireless), and the merger of Sprint with Nextel Communications. These mergers sought to enhance pricing power and reduce customer "churn," or defection of customers from one provider to another.[2]

Economies of Scale

Providers capturing the highest share of customers in a given market will generally benefit from the lowest costs per customer. Businesses gain economies of scale when they can spread their fixed costs over a wider number of paying customers. From an operational perspective, outsourcing major cost drivers and standardizing product designs are key drivers of economies of scale. When key activities cannot be outsourced, an investment emphasis on automation enables the business to do more with fewer labor costs. The more customers the business serves, the faster it reduces its fixed unit costs.

Caterpillar's continued success in dominating numerous global markets for locomotives (its EMD unit was acquired from General Motors), construction equipment, and specialized mining machinery is testament to the company's focus on attaining economies of scale in its key operational activities. Within its plants, Caterpillar has invested billions of dollars in automating its key metal bending, forging, stamping, fabrication, and assembly activities. At the same time, Caterpillar also works closely with its key suppliers to selectively outsource component design and production of cost-sensitive, standardized parts (e.g., axles, gears, pumps) where it is more economically feasible to do so. Over the past 30 years, Caterpillar's scale-driven strategy has enabled it to not only fend off major challenges from Japanese construction equipment giant Komatsu, but also to gain market share from smaller companies such as John Deere, Samsung, and CNH (Case New

Holland). Caterpillar now faces a major test of its scale-driven strategy as it seeks to take on fast-growing Chinese competitors in their home market (e.g., Sany Heavy Industries).

Leveraged Bargaining Power

Consolidators can enhance their profitability by strengthening their bargaining power *vis à vis* their suppliers and their buyers. For example, the continued high profitability of managed care firms, such as Cigna and WellPoint, stems from their ability to share costs with both their suppliers (e.g., physician practices, hospital chains, pharmacy benefit managers, drug firms), and their customers (employee benefit plans run by businesses on behalf of their workers). To increase their bargaining power, both firms acquired rivals to reduce the number of competitors (e.g., Cigna's recent acquisition of Medicare specialist Healthspring; WellPoint's numerous serial acquisitions of Blue Cross/Blue Shield providers across many states) to increase the number of patients covered in a market region. This has enabled the managed care giants to better control their costs by slowing down the rate of cost increases imposed by suppliers in their respective networks.[3]

Primacy of Cost-Efficient Operations

As we will soon discover in greater detail, the central pillar of the consolidator's business strategy is the overriding priority of cost efficiency. Consolidators can identify, exploit, and capture cost efficiency through a number of different methods. Some consolidators will spend heavily on automating processes so that every possible economic cost is squeezed to its maximum. This includes such cost drivers as inventory holding cost, waiting time, work-in-process, transport, labor overtime, and even perishability. One has to look no further than Wal-Mart Stores to see how the dominant discount and grocery retailer has made cost efficiency a mantra.

Similarly, consolidators can run extremely lean, outsourced operations that become almost "virtual" in their form. For example, Dell became synonymous with outsourced, built-to-order production of personal computers during the 1990s. Today, Vizio is a leading producer of flat-screen LCD television sets. It produces none of the components that it assembles and sells under the Vizio brand.

Other consolidators systematically build enormous state-of-the-art plants that make it impossible for other competitors to duplicate, simply because the economics of the operation is so daunting. For example, Pohang Iron and Steel Company of Korea (aka Posco) has constructed such enormous, massive steel mills that it is the world's cost leader in integrated steel production. Its mills are even lower cost than those of neighboring Nippon Steel's modern plants in Japan. Similarly, Sysco, a food distributor, has built six regional distribution centers, each of 550,000 square feet, across the United States to drive down its distribution costs to its major customer, the food service company ARAMARK. Likewise, despite the ever-rising and daunting technical hurdles that it must overcome, Intel continues to invest billions of dollars in leading-edge microprocessor plants to preclude almost every other semiconductor firm from entering the business. Each Intel plant costs upwards of $4 billion and produces millions of state-of-the-art microprocessors and other chips. The investment is so huge that almost every other semiconductor company in the world has stopped short of following Intel's steps. Only Samsung Electronics has stayed committed to building even larger plants for its own microchip needs.

Strategic Issues for Consolidators

As noted from these examples, Consolidators from all types of industries face enormous challenges resulting from their inability to grow at their previous fast rates. Because of the zero-sum nature of slow or no-growth industries, Consolidators' gains in market share are almost impossible to attain without bruising battles with other firms, most often through price wars. Unfortunately, customers become accustomed to these price wars and will rarely pay anything but a discounted price, especially for a standardized product that is largely indistinguishable from its rivals. Moreover, many businesses will not have reached the point where they have paid down their fixed costs, often in the form of long-term debt. This encumbrance further reduces their strategic flexibility to craft new product offerings to avoid the onslaught of further price wars.

Central to the Consolidators' sustainable competitive advantage is the pursuit of cost-efficiency in every aspect of their operations. This search for cost-efficiency cannot come at the expense of product quality, however. Consolidators must preserve their brand equity (and therefore some degree of attractiveness to its customers) while simultaneously looking for every possible way to streamline, standardize, and render operations consistent across the organization. Consolidators tend to be large businesses that grew in earlier time periods through expansion into new markets, new product lines, and even through acquisitions that complemented their offerings. As a result, the Consolidator is likely to own a portfolio of different types of businesses, each with its own way of doing things. When previous growth rates were high, the business focused primarily on responding quickly to customers' needs, designing or developing new product variations to sell to different market segments, and hiring large numbers of employees to staff the expanding business. This pattern of fast growth also translated into a business imperative where cost efficiency and consistency of operations were relegated to more secondary considerations. The key strategic issues facing Consolidators are depicted in Table 6.1.

Consider, for example, the rapid growth of ConAgra, a leading U.S. food processing company, through the 1970s and 1980s. During those years, ConAgra grew by acquiring hundreds of smaller food companies that were either undervalued, poorly managed turnaround candidates, or serving small niches. These included such well-known brand names as Butterball (turkey meat), Hunt-Wesson (ketchup and cooking oils),

---

Table 6.1 Key Strategic Issues for Consolidators

- Execute cost efficiency discipline in every activity
- Leverage economies of scale in operations and procurement
- Pursue standardized approaches when serving customers
- Maintain consistency of operations

Armour (processed meats), Orville Redenbacher (popcorn), Hebrew National (hot dogs), and Swift (hams and other processed meats). The food processing industry began to slow down but still continued to grow at rates faster than that of U.S. population growth. By the mid-1990s, however, ConAgra faced growing pressures to streamline its widely dispersed base of operations. Increasingly powerful buyers, spurred by a merger wave among grocery retailers, began to demand major price concessions from ConAgra and other food processors. In addition, the entry of Wal-Mart and Target Stores into the grocery retailing business further depressed margins for ConAgra and its rivals. Wal-Mart used its enormous buying power to demand further price reductions as well as added services from them. At the same time, a growing percentage of U.S. families began consuming a larger proportion of their meals outside the home. This dramatically cut into the growth opportunities for processed foods.

In response to these industry pressures, ConAgra implemented a series of strategic initiatives designed to lower the firm's total cost structure. First, ConAgra introduced an internal strategic sourcing plan that compelled the different food product lines to coordinate and leverage the purchase of key packaging materials to capture greater economies of scale. Second, senior management began to evaluate internal business units on how well they cooperated with each other to identify new cost-savings measures that would translate into total system-wide savings. This major change in incentive design proved initially difficult for ConAgra's managers to accept, since they were previously assessed on the basis of how fast they grew their product lines and market positions. Each product manager was expected to uncover new cost savings opportunities, including ways to speed up the packaging of food portions in factories. Third, ConAgra introduced team-selling among its sales force to ensure that they could negotiate more effectively with its buyers, the large grocery store chains that already had begun to consolidate among themselves. Team-selling enabled ConAgra to mitigate the effect of excessive demands for extreme discounts demanded by buyers. Fourth, ConAgra insisted that each and every subsequent major capital investment meet stringent financial return criteria to ensure that all other opportunities to squeeze out costs were not overlooked. Finally, ConAgra sold off those businesses that no longer fit. Earlier investments in agricultural services, large-scale refrigeration technologies, and other pre-existing businesses were either completely sold or dramatically reduced in size.[4]

General Electric has begun to fundamentally change the way it trains its future leaders to deal with the simultaneous pressures of globalization and industry consolidation. Instead of transferring managers to work across an array of different GE business for only a few years, GE is now encouraging its managerial talent to gain greater depth and experience within a line of business focused on a single industry. This major strategic transition represents a big turnaround for the giant company that earned a well-deserved reputation for training and developing legions of "generalist" managers skilled at applying their business acumen to a variety of different business situations. The reason for this paradigm change is clear. GE's preference for strategic depth in its leadership mirrors the firm's quest for greater business focus rather than a wide breadth of operations. For each of GE's businesses, the opportunities for domestic growth in the United States remain limited. Even when GE looks abroad for renewed growth, it already faces established rivals entrenched in their respective domestic markets, or it must become even more cost-effective than emerging market competitors in such fast-growth arenas as China, India, Brazil, Australia and elsewhere. In other words, even though global markets are growing faster than those in the U.S., pressures to consolidate are already taking root in each of GE's foreign business operations too. To respond to these pressures of fiercer competition and tighter budgets for capital expenditures among buyers, GE wants its future leaders to be able to better understand and articulate their customers' needs, translate new technology into new products faster, and deepen their base of specialized knowledge. Leaders with only a cursory understanding of a key technology or customers' needs will not be able to develop the kind of distinctive products that attract and retain customers. This new focus on specialized career development parallels GE's recent moves in each of its major businesses to further consolidate its operations. It has exited those where it no longer can be a dominant player, such as media (NBC Universal), plastics (sold to Saudi Basic Industries), and insurance (spun off as a separate business, Genworth Financial).[5]

The economic imperatives of industry maturity can wreak havoc on large businesses that do not consolidate. Although once feared as technological juggernauts that would crush any U.S. or European company in consumer electronics, many of today's Japanese giants are fast losing market share to fiercer, more cost-efficient South Korean, Chinese, and Southeast Asian rivals. Legendary companies, including Sharp, Panasonic, Toshiba, Ricoh, and Hitachi, were once synonymous with beautifully designed, high-quality electronics products. Yet, over the past 20 years, these firms largely missed the boat as new rivals became increasingly competitive in developing and producing their own indigenous products, often at much lower cost and with similarly advanced features. For example, Samsung and LG of Korea developed their own deep-core competencies in such fields as microelectronics, LCD displays, semiconductors, and other components that laid the foundation for their own explosive entry onto the global marketplace in the late 1990s. Yet, most Japanese firms failed to recognize how fast the consumer electronics industry matured. Ironically, Japanese consumer electronics firms cannot match the cost-efficiency of their South Korean and Chinese rivals, with the result that Panasonic, Sharp, Toshiba, and Hitachi have lost both market share and mind share among customers.[6]

Likewise, within the United States, the bankruptcy filing by AMR Corporation in November 2011, the parent of American Airlines, partially stems from the air carrier's unwillingness or inability to use its once-leading position in the industry to consolidate operations over the past decade. Considered the largest U.S. airline by some key industry measures in 2000, American Airlines fell behind UnitedContinental Holdings and Delta Airlines after both of these carriers merged with their respective acquisition targets. Over the past decade, American's "legacy" costs grew, including such cost drivers as employee benefits, unionized labor costs, pension liabilities, and the revamping of core hub operations, in addition to meteoric rises in fuel costs. Conversely, both

United and Delta took advantage of earlier bankruptcy petitions to negotiate much more favorable labor cost contracts and to merge with similarly sized carriers in order to form the number one and two carriers in the industry. Both carriers now possess greater pricing power and reach than that of American. In response, American Airlines and US Airways merged to form the largest U.S.-based carrier to capture economies of scale.[7]

Arenas

Consolidators typically aim to capture and sustain large market share positions. Offering highly standardized products, Consolidators acquire customers through aggressive pricing and a reputation for offering lines that are consistent, if not necessarily earth-shattering or of the finest quality. Because they have been in the industry for an extended time, Consolidators develop strong sources of knowledge and benefit from experience-curve effects that enable them to transfer expertise and skills from one set of products to another. Examples of experience-curve effects include an understanding of, and methods for, dealing with a certain type of buyer, process improvements and refinements that enable a business to lower unit costs in a successive product generation, and sources of internal learning that enable the firm to "routinize" its activities to reduce waiting time, work-in-process, or other latent inefficiencies.

In the consumer packaged goods and personal care products industries, Procter & Gamble has made strides to understand the needs of a growing base of retail customers who feel increasingly pinched by a weak U.S. economy. Well-known for its numerous businesses including Tide detergents, Ivory Soap, Febreze air fresheners, Bounty paper towels, and Charmin bathroom paper, P&G has built strong competitive advantages over the decades by serving middle-class customers with reliable, dependable, and trustworthy products. P&G's focus on the middle class enabled it to build 24 billion-dollar brands. Of P&G's $83.6 billion in revenues in 2012, these key brands contribute a disproportionate 70 per cent of sales. P&G has taken two different approaches to competing in the personal care products arena.

Along one dimension, P&G pushes each of its major brands to find product line extensions that will bolster market share gains by identifying new uses for the core product. For example, the Febreze line of air fresheners, which launched in 1998 and recently hit $1 billion in revenue, expanded to include specialty fragrances for cars, sportswear, pets, carpets, and allergens. The original Febreze product was designed as a fabric treatment to freshen curtains, clothing, sofas, and other furniture items that could not be cleaned in a washing machine using Tide detergent.[8]

To gain efficiencies, P&G is now also developing a series of product variants that have some of the company's most advanced or leading-edge attributes removed. For example, to cater to a growing number of cash-strapped consumers, P&G modified its Charmin and Bounty paper products lines to include a Charmin Basic and a Bounty Basic variety. These less expensive products are designed to fulfill the needs of consumers who ordinarily would have purchased P&G's mainstream products, but who simply can no longer afford them. To prevent these consumers from defecting to other consumer products firms, such as Church & Dwight, S. C. Johnson & Son, and Unilever, P&G has also put more advertising dollars into such products as Cheer, Gain, and Era—products that are designed to protect the Tide and Downy brands.[9]

Although P&G continues to spend heavily advertising and promoting all of its products, it has strengthened its overall product portfolio by divesting itself of products that no longer contribute significantly to either continued unit volume growth or profitability. At the same time, P&G has acquired major businesses via which it can further enhance the acquisition's growth prospects and market share gains. In particular, P&G has steadily exited from competing in the food industry arena, where extremely thin margins and brutal competition from larger and better-funded competitors make it impossible for P&G to sustain its competitive advantage. In its most recent divestiture, P&G sought to sell its Pringles line of canned potato chips to Diamond Foods for $1.5 billion, although complications with the deal enabled Kellogg to purchase Pringles in late 2012 to complement its own array of cereals, cookies, and other food lines. Over the past decade, P&G has sold off its Folgers Coffee, Sunny Delight orange juice, Jif peanut butter, and Crisco cooking oil businesses.[10] Concurrently, P&G spent close to $80 billion acquiring such well-known brands as Gillette (shaving care products), Duracell (batteries as part of the Gillette transaction), Clairol and Wella (hair care products), and Iams (high-end dog and cat food). Many of these businesses enable P&G to strengthen its ability to cross-sell products and to negotiate better terms with larger retail buyers, such as Wal-Mart, Target, and Costco. For example, the company is looking at ways to combine its Pantene, Oil of Olay and Gillette products to devise a new, "friendlier" type of razor for the female market.[11]

The Hon Hai Precision Industry Company is probably the single most important electronics manufacturer in the world that most people have never heard of. Based in Taiwan, but operating several gargantuan fabrication and assembly plants throughout China, Hon Hai (also known as Foxconn for a group of affiliated units) is the world's largest contract electronics manufacturer. Started in 1974 as a small producer of black-and-white televisions, Hon Hai now has over a million workers in its vast array of manufacturing plants. Hon Hai makes and assembles hugely popular products for such well-known companies as Apple, Hewlett-Packard, Sony Electronics, Microsoft, Cisco Systems, Nintendo, and Motorola, among others. Hon Hai currently does not design any of the products that it manufactures for its business customers. Its enormous factories endow it with global economies of scale, and when combined with extremely lean and agile supply chains, give Hon Hai tremendous pricing influence over the consumer electronics, cell phone, video game console, and telecommunications equipment industries. Hon Hai's global manufacturing competence gives it strong leverage over the successful timing of product releases also. Other contract electronics manufacturers competing with Hon Hai include names Flextronics, Solectron, and Celestica—all of whom seek to emulate Hon Hai's scale-driven, cost-efficient operations.

Hon Hai's growing clout has started to gain many firms' notice, albeit belatedly. With rising cash reserves, the company has taken a

10 per cent stake in Sharp Corporation, lending the Japanese giant an important helping hand in resuscitating the proud producer of highly advanced LCD screens and solar panels. Hon Hai will now become the largest shareholder in Sharp and will gain access to its cutting-edge technology for use in its own products. It is also expected to buy up to half of all of Sharp's most advanced LCD screens. Although the relationship has become contentious, this long-term supply arrangement enables Sharp to help stabilize itself after failing to consolidate its own operations with other Japanese electronics giants during the past decade. Pricing for consumer electronics fell but most Japanese giants believed they could rely on their own manufacturing operations, none of which made rapidly growing and popular products like smartphones, tablets, and other advanced devices.[12]

Yum Brands is one of the world's largest restaurant companies. Yet, in the past few years, Yum has felt ever more squeezed by further consolidating pressures in the U.S. restaurant industry. To recapture its initiative, Yum has attempted to regain its balance by refocusing on its core three restaurant units—Pizza Hut, KFC, and Taco Bell. In January 2011, Yum announced that it would sell off its Long John Silver's and A&W restaurant chains to improve the competitiveness of Taco Bell. Throughout 2011, Yum has initiated steps to partner with PepsiCo's Frito-Lay unit to create "Doritos Locos Tacos," a new product that uses Doritos chips as taco shells. It has also started working with celebrity chefs to introduce a line of edible Mexican food bowls that can be sold at higher prices in Taco Bell restaurants. In addition, Yum wants to simultaneously reposition its KFC line to emphasize the freshness of its chicken products and to expand KFC's breakfast options. Yet, the real opportunity for Yum to continue growing its earnings is the vast opportunities it faces in China and other emerging markets. Yum has ironically become one of China's biggest producers of fast-food dumplings, a staple that the Chinese population craves and represents one of Yum's biggest sources of growth in its global markets. Yum is also developing a line of low-cost breakfasts in China, and is experimenting with a fast-food concept known as "East Dawning" in China.[13] A summary of the arena-related issues facing Consolidators is shown in Table 6.2.

Table 6.2 Key Arena Issues for Consolidators
• Pursue large market share • Exploit long-held experience to improve efficiencies • Serve a wide geography

Vehicles

Consolidators can employ a number of vehicles to further strengthen their position within a mature industry. Related acquisitions of other businesses from other firms enable Consolidators to rapidly gain market share and strengthen their competitive postures. These moves, however, can create other tradeoffs related to how best to integrate these operations. Managed health-care firms, such as Aetna, Cigna, and WellPoint, which have grown extensively through acquiring smaller health-care businesses, have confronted some of these issues in recent years as they face the challenges of integrating different health plans into a more standardized set of benefit offerings to their large employer customer base.

Consolidators can also pursue continued and sustained investment in their core businesses to further expand and strengthen their market positions. For example, a continued commitment to build ever-larger and more modern factories at Intel and Caterpillar represent important market signals that demonstrate to rivals their commitment to aggressively defend their market positions. Other Consolidators may take a completely different approach to improving their competitiveness. They may choose to further outsource even more of their activities to more agile or lower-cost providers in attempting to preserve profitability. Thus, Consolidators can pursue any number of vehicles to strengthen their businesses.

Micron Technology may be America's remaining memory chip producer, but it is fast becoming the number two player in this consolidating industry. Second only to Samsung, Micron recently announced that it would purchase its Japanese rival, Elpida Memory for $2.5 billion. Elpida itself is the product of a three-way tie-up among NEC, Mitsubishi Electric, and Hitachi's memory chip businesses. Elpida was formed in response to the growing pressures that each of the three Japanese electronics giants faced when they realized that none of them on their own had the requisite economies of scale needed to invest and compete in this volatile industry. Micron's purchase of Elpida will give it access not only to the large Japanese market, but also to significantly advanced technology and capacity made possible by Elpida's previous investments in new types of manufacturing. Micron's management noted that the Elpida purchase will give it new capacity that cost it less than a third of what it would take to build it from scratch.[14]

Amazon's rapid rise as a retail Consolidator can be traced to a number of key moves that the e-retailing giant made in the past several years. Based on its continuous investment in state-of-the-art delivery and new processing technologies, Amazon can dramatically lower the cost of serving its customers in such a way that it can potentially and completely displace pre-existing rivals. Amazon is spearheading efforts to use its technological prowess and wide customer reach to consolidate almost any sector that it touches. Companies such as Apple, Barnes & Noble, and Netflix are beginning to feel the heat of Amazon's low-cost entry into their respective businesses.[15]

How has Amazon created such strong advantages? First, Amazon has steadily invested in building its own warehouses and order-fulfillment centers, regardless of how these steps impacted short-term profitability. Amazon believes that it must continue to invest in larger, more modern facilities to support its rapid growth and expansion into all types of product categories that it sells on its website. In 2012, Amazon built 20 new fulfillment centers alone, for a total of 89 centers system-wide and expects to continue building more in 2013.[16]

Second, Amazon has no hesitation spending large sums on product R&D that enables it to challenge market leaders such as Apple and Netflix in tablets and online movies respectively. Amazon has sought to become a one-stop shopping place for all types of merchandise, with its most recent emphasis on digital offerings. It has made major strides in providing e-books and e-music as it diversifies away from its once-core business of selling print books and CDs over the Internet. It lays claim to 60 per cent of the book market, 23 per cent of the video market, and 20 per cent of the music market, too. It continues its retailing transformation to become an online digital provider that blends access to movie and music content with its own-branded devices. Now, with its Kindle line of products taking firm root in the marketplace, Amazon recently introduced a music and video-playing digital device known as Kindle Fire. Amazon is aiming to take the best of Apple's product features and replicate them onto its own gadgets. It will also compete with Barnes & Noble's Nook, a low-cost e-reader that also offers a color screen and Web access.[17] Built on a simplified version of Google's Android operating system, the Kindle Fire can take advantage of Amazon's previous steps of accumulating a vast library of digital content of e-books, music, and now, movies.[18] Amazon has also struck important deals with several large publishing houses to ensure that popular magazine titles are available on the Kindle Fire as well.[19] The first generation of Kindle Fire is priced significantly lower than Apple's iPad—$199 versus $499.[20] Jeff Bezos, CEO of Amazon, regards each generation of Kindle and the Kindle Fire as nothing more than lower-cost and more convenient ways to enter the world of digital media and content.[21]

In the fast-converging digital arena, Amazon intends to make its presence and its low-cost operations felt. In 2011, Amazon began to offer its Prime customers movies and television shows for instant viewing over the Internet. Amazon hopes that its video-streaming business will encourage customers to purchase or rent some of the 90,000 movies and television shows that it already has in its vast library. This move also enables Amazon to directly challenge Netflix on its pricing terms as well, since the $79 that Amazon Prime customers pay is still cheaper than the $7.99 a month offered to Netflix's subscribers.[22] Ironically, Netflix has begun using Amazon's cloud storage systems to enhance its video-streaming technology, even though the two firms continue to battle for the attention of broadcasters and viewers.[23]

Third, Amazon has continued to ramp up investment in making its warehouses—both digital and physical—even more cost-efficient. In the digital arena, Amazon has become an important voice in the "cloud computing" technology environment, where companies including IBM, EMC, and Dell offer corporate clients a vast amount of computing and data storage in a virtual setting. In short, companies that use "cloud computing" can effectively gain access to low-cost, vast data storage through off-site, outsourced servers built and run by large computer giants. Amazon has become an important influence in shaping how cloud computing will impact its vast digital library and its "big data" customer operations. In contrast to Apple, which looks at its devices as the primary value driver to customers, Amazon believes that "the cloud" is more important than the device or appliance used to enter the Internet. Amazon already has close to a 20 per cent share of the cloud computing market and is rapidly growing. In this post-web view of technology, Amazon is working with a number of computer industry partners to make future use of the Internet "device-free" (e.g., no need for keyboards or PCs) to access its warehouses of digital content. In its physical warehouses, Amazon recently spent $775 million to acquire Kiva Systems, a leading provider of robotics used to manage and coordinate inventories within factories and warehouses. Kiva's robots are designed to move products from pre-set locations on warehouse shelves directly to where workers pack the ordered products along the warehouse's conveyor belt. These laser-guided robots save workers the time and physical effort needed to locate and fetch the inventory to fulfill a customer's order. Kiva Systems represent Amazon's second biggest acquisition to date, after its purchase of Zappos.com for $895 million in 2009.[24]

United Parcel Service (UPS) is using acquisitions to compete with one FedEx in the package-delivery and logistics business. In March 2012, UPS announced that it would purchase the important Dutch delivery firm TNT Express for nearly $7 billion in order to strengthen its operations in Europe and Asia. TNT Express will play an important role for UPS as it seeks to streamline and consolidate its shipping routes across the two oceans. Although UPS is famous for running an extremely tight ship, it has not fared as well at creating new businesses from within. The TNT acquisition will enable UPS

Table 6.3 Key Vehicle Issues for Consolidators
• Acquire other businesses to reinforce scale benefits • Interest in new processes and methods to lower costs • Outsource non-core activities

to blend the best practices of both companies to create an even stronger UPS. Ironically, UPS's acquisition of TNT may also help FedEx, since it removes another player in a rapidly consolidating market. The primary vehicles used by Consolidators to support their strategies are shown in Table 6.3.

Staging

Consolidators typically look at identifying and building economies of scale in a core activity (usually one highly sensitive to fixed costs or high volumes) and then leverage that experience to further capture even greater scale economies in a related or neighboring activity. Consider, for example, the rapid ascendancy of Samsung Electronics over the past 15 years. Once thought of as a company that makes "me-too" products that imitate other firms' leading product designs, Samsung Electronics has transformed its dominant position in making highly standardized memory chips into a leading global provider of LCD flat-screen television sets and advanced home appliances. It is engaged in a ferocious fight with Apple as the number two provider of advanced smartphones in 2012.

In the 1990s, Samsung grew from a start-up into one of the world's largest manufacturers of advanced memory chips. The memory chip industry is a notoriously volatile one in which cycles swing to extreme degrees of "feast or famine." Yet, as other once-leading semiconductor industry players (e.g., Motorola, Texas Instruments, ST Microelectronics) exited the arena, Samsung continued to invest in state-of-the-art plants that gave it significantly greater economies of scale with each successive product generation. Ultimately, even the largest industry players, such as Toshiba, NEC, IBM, Mitsubishi Electric, and Hitachi, left the industry, leaving Samsung as the number one player in memory chips. It now controls 50 per cent of the world's memory chip business, and has a highly enviable and lucrative position within the semiconductor industry.[25] With its dominant position (and growing pricing power), Samsung leveraged its hard-won technical skills in miniaturization and manufacturing to move into the early digital cell phone, television, and home appliance businesses by providing the electronic "brains" that make these products work—both for its own-branded products, as well as for other competing firms seeking a low-cost chip supply for their own needs. Samsung thus leveraged its cost-efficiency skills learned from making memory chips to vertically integrate into more profitable products, thereby staging its entry into the consumer-branded products that are now in high demand among customers worldwide. Samsung also hopes to move up the semiconductor value chain by applying its miniaturization skills to new types of more profitable micro-controller and logic chips.

Samsung was initially slow to develop smartphones, but now its Galaxy line of phones and tablets are beginning to challenge Apple's offerings in a serious way. Since it is a maker of advanced chips for both its own Galaxy products, as well as for Apple and other rivals, it captures even more momentum in that market. Samsung competes very differently from Apple (which is much more of a Trendsetter in its business) along several important dimensions. First, unlike Apple, which emphasizes sleek, elegant product design and high unit profitability over revenue gains, Samsung pursues economies of scale in every activity. It has already overtaken Nokia to become the number two provider of smartphones in 2012. Already, other smartphone makers have begun to reel under the weight of Samsung's enormous economies of scale in production and distribution. The Taiwan-based HTC saw its market share plummet from 11 per cent to 2 per cent as new Samsung models undercut its prices.[26] Samsung is a fast-follower that places lots of bets across a series of products by selling its own branded products and providing critical components for its rivals. Ironically, even though Apple prevailed in an important court case protecting its patents from Samsung, it continues to be a major customer for one of Samsung's

LCD and OLED component divisions, which make the touch-screen technologies possible on smartphones.[27]

Second, while Apple (a Trendsetter) developed its own line of iPhone and iPad software, Samsung has relied heavily on licensing Google's Android system to serve as the complement to its chip hardware. In attempting to leapfrog Apple, Samsung originally embraced a variety of smartphone operating systems software, and eventually chose Android for its technical versatility and rapid market acceptance. This is a page from Samsung's playbook in the past as well, when the company placed a wide array of bets on competing Trendsetting industry standards in the VCR and DVD industries, only to choose a "winning" standard after it reached a critical mass of popularity in the marketplace.[28]

Finally, Samsung is also seeking to break free in the long term from its reliance on Android by developing its own software capabilities. Samsung wants to become a software powerhouse itself and design next-generation applications and operating systems for future smartphones, tablets, and other hybrid electronic personal appliances. This step is also reminiscent of another page in Samsung's playbook—this time in consumer appliances. When Samsung originally wanted to enter the microwave oven business in the mid-1980s, it worked closely with General Electric to learn how to build these products. GE would provide the technical designs to Samsung, and the ambitious, aspiring Korean upstart would then reverse-engineer and rapidly build the systems according to GE's specifications. Ultimately, Samsung would become so cost-efficient in making microwave ovens that it began to compete against GE itself, eventually displacing it from the vast majority of U.S. households, even if the final product still bore the GE nameplate. Later, Samsung would learn how to build even more advanced versions of microwave ovens from Maytag, before turning the tables on the Iowa-based appliance company (now part of Whirlpool Corporation).

There is little doubt, then, that Samsung will try to leverage the skills and capabilities learned from working with Android to challenge Google on its own software turf sometime in the near future. Its newest operating system, called "Bada," will seek to gain the best performance

Table 6.4 Key Staging Issues for Consolidators
• Adopt a wait-and-see approach before committing to a new product/service • Leverage scale in one market or activity to enter a neighboring one • Avoid being first-to-market

features from competing software offerings. Samsung will open up its emerging Bada platforms to software experts from outside the company to improve the system's performance, and also allow other firms to modify Bada's source code for free. Samsung hopes that this strategy will boost growth for its own software and ultimately reduce its dependence on Google.[29] Table 6.4 highlights the primary ways in which Consolidators stage their activities to support their strategies.

Distinction

Consolidators find it particularly difficult to retain customers' loyalty over time periods, largely because they can easily switch from one provider to another based on pricing, convenience, and availability of products or services. Price wars also complicate Consolidators' efforts to maintain industry discipline. Products and their features are standardized and astute customers can easily compare each firm's value proposition. Decisions normally turn on price. Consolidators should avoid price wars because they all lose. They can, however, attain distinction mostly through the long-term proven consistency and value that their products offer to their customers. Attaining product consistency requires an organizational and operational set-up that focuses on achieving and replicating uniform product quality time and time again.

Consider, for example, the near-obsession that UPS devotes to refining and perfecting each and every process that underpins its logistics business. The company invests tens of millions of dollars each year into state-of-the-art information and order-fulfillment technologies that enable employees, vendors, and customers to track the status of their package shipments at any time. Most recently, the company is now investing in a three-dimensional bar-code tracking system that can read packages from all six sides as they move rapidly down a conveyor belt, after which they are sorted by size, shape, and delivery destination. Process excellence is so important to UPS that it even has a "university" dedicated to learning and applying best practices to all aspects of its organization, too. UPS drivers in particular are trained in over 100 exacting procedures, including the need to avoid left-turns where possible and to pre-place packages in the truck in such a way that heavier packages come out first in order to save time.

McDonald's is perhaps the most recognized restaurant brand around the world. Although best known for its wide selection of low-priced hamburgers, French fries, shakes, and other beverages, McDonald's has relied heavily on sourcing the new menu ideas from its "living network" of suppliers, owner-operators (franchisees), and food experts. In particular, some of McDonald's biggest hits came from franchisees who thought up a slew of winners, including the Big Mac, Fish-Filet sandwiches, Quarter Pounders, and other items. Franchisees also are responsible for much of the evolution in the design of McDonald's restaurants, too. In 1962, a Denver owner-operator introduced the first interior dining room. Five years later, the famous stylized double arch architectural design became omnipresent. In 1968, an Illinois operator introduced a French-style, four-sided roof that became the standard for almost all stand-alone restaurants.[30]

In the United States today, the firm has introduced a variety of new menu items ranging from those designed to appeal to the value customer (seeking food costing less than $1) to higher-priced salads and even bowls of oatmeal for workers on the go. The emphasis today remains on delivering "compelling customer conveniences" at a low cost, no matter where the customer may be located worldwide. Delivering food by motorcycle has become common practice in densely populated cities in China, South Korea, and Egypt. Globally, McDonald's is updating and redesigning many of its signature restaurants, and extending operating hours to serve people working outside traditional office hours.[31]

Over the decades, McDonald's has methodically searched for better ways of cooking and serving its food. The company is always experimenting with methods for reducing waiting time for customers, keeping the food fresh, redesigning the kitchen to improve safety as well as custom orders, and continually upgrading its offerings in response to changing market demand. McDonald's singular focus on introducing, improving, and making its food consistent drives its total strategy. Behind each restaurant is a highly synchronized series of steps that every employee must learn and follow in order to prepare and deliver food to customers in the shortest possible waiting time.

Delivering food consistency with every single order demands a system that yields unerring process efficiency. In an ironic way, McDonald's has perfected and implemented a total quality improvement system that emulates the best Japanese practitioners, including Toyota, Sony, and Canon. Every variable that can negatively impact food quality must be identified and eliminated. The more variation removed, the better the ultimate product. Providing the most desirable but consistently produced food is at the heart of McDonald's system. Carl Sewell, CEO of Sewell Automotive of Dallas, says it best:

> When McDonald's began their quest to serve the perfect French fry every time, there were no national standards for potatoes. The U.S. Department of Agriculture didn't have a grading system which said: This is a good potato, that one's better, and the one over there is awful. In addition, no one knew exactly how hot the grease used to fry the potato should be, or how you could guarantee that temperature would remain constant during cooking, or how the potatoes should be stored to keep them from spoiling. By the time McDonald's finished, they had helped establish the quality standards for the Department of Agriculture. They knew what kind of soil the potatoes should be grown in to achieve the consistency they wanted. They even created their own frying equipment to ensure that the potatoes cooked the same way every time. To me this story exemplifies customer service. By devoting all that time and attention to the ways potatoes are grown, stored, and cooked, McDonald's has virtually guaranteed that the fries they serve you will be good every time.[32]

McDonald's continues to work with its major suppliers, Simplot and McCain, to purchase huge volumes of potatoes grown according to its exacting standards.

Intel is another example of a firm achieving distinction through following rules for process excellence. Intel is the number one semiconductor producer in the world, and unlike many of its rivals, it prefers to produce all of its leading-edge microprocessors and other state-of-the-art chips in-house. The company has six ultra-modern chip "fabs" (two in Oregon; one each in Arizona, New Mexico, Ireland, and Israel) that push the limits of science in both production and circuit design. Under former CEO Andy Grove, a Hungarian émigré who bet the company's future on the now-famous x86 chip architecture, Intel believed that the only way it could control and maintain the extreme quality of its chips was to self-manufacture.[33] Controlling manufacturing enables Intel to raise the bar for continuous improvement and unrelenting process excellence. As Intel's microprocessors become increasingly dense, its engineers are able to work in parallel— ever more intricate chips demand ever more complex steps to build them. A deep understanding of the manufacturing process gives Intel distinction in identifying new ways to design next-generation chips that overcome the limits of existing scientific and technological constraints. By controlling each and every aspect of both chip design and factory design, Intel leads the world in producing and delivering ever more powerful microprocessors and other chips to its customers. The critical sources of distinction supporting a Consolidator's strategy are found in Table 6.5.

Table 6.5 Ways to Achieve Distinction for Consolidators

- Earn a reputation for consistency in customers' minds
- Develop processes that yield uniform product quality
- Constantly benchmark against more cost-efficient firms
- Avoid price wars if possible

Economic Logic

The pursuit of economies of scale and process excellence represents the pillars of Consolidators' economic logic. Brutal competition, savvy customers, and high fixed costs conspire to depress Consolidators' profit margins. In many industries, margins are so razor-thin that even once large, prosperous businesses run the risk of financial ruin as even bigger firms gobble up their market share. Consider, for example, the current travails facing such U.S. grocery retailers as Supervalu, Inc. and Safeway. Although both companies were once industry leaders and grew through acquisition to expand their national reach during the 1990s, neither firm could match the cost efficiencies of even more powerful and larger firms such as Wal-Mart Stores and Target. From 2010 to 2012, increasingly pinched customers and more intense price-based competition has pushed Supervalu (the holding company for Albertson's, Acme, Jewel, Osco) to the precipice of bankruptcy. Private equity firms are now seeking to purchase various pieces of Supervalu to restructure its underlying business cost structures. Because the overall size of the total market available to all competitors has become a fixed pie (as a result of slow or no growth in the United States), market share gains for any one firm must generally come at the expense of another. Expanding a Consolidator's profit margin will primarily come from further efforts to reduce total costs internally and to win market share from rivals externally.

This compelling economic logic has shaped and driven General Electric's mantra of seeking to become Number One or Number Two in each of its business lines. GE's strategy for competing in mature businesses is simple: grab enough market share to become Number One or Two or exit the business completely. By becoming Number One or Two, a GE business can gain the sustained benefits of economies of scale and withstand the inherent and inevitable cyclical swings that impact volume production. In addition, the GE business obtains greater bargaining power and leverage in working with its vendors and buyers; this helps to mitigate the effects of destructive price-based competition. Attempting to buttress a weak or small business with few growth prospects in a mature industry ultimately diverts and wastes capital that could be devoted to enhancing process efficiency and cost-reduction efforts in a stronger business. This guiding principle, formulated and executed by Jack Welch during his tenure as CEO, has helped propel GE to become one of the most valuable companies in the United States for many years during his stewardship. To pursue industry leadership, GE has used a combination of external acquisitions to grow core businesses (e.g., power generation, energy, mining, medical equipment) and selective divestitures to exit from those arenas where it could not attain strong market power (e.g., media, plastics, certain defense businesses, consumer electronics, insurance). In those businesses that GE retained, senior management set and executed ever-higher benchmarks for operational improvements using management techniques and programs, including Six Sigma (statistical process improvements), Black Belts (GE's training methodology for identifying and removing process inefficiencies), and tight financial metrics.

Even retailing giant Wal-Mart has relearned the lesson that it must remain focused on its overriding priority of cost efficiency as its economic logic. From 2009 to 2011, Wal-Mart faced a prolonged sales slump at its U.S.-based stores as customers began to think that the company no longer offered the best prices. Since its inception, Wal-Mart has long promoted a policy of "everyday low prices" on everything from apparel to sporting goods to automotive supplies, and in recent years, to food as well. Wal-Mart typically avoided sales gimmicks that tricked customers into visiting a store, only to find that few products were truly price-competitive. In hoping to avoid the brutal price wars that define retailing, several years ago Wal-Mart attempted to remodel its stores and to offer an expanded line of higher-priced merchandise to reach higher-income customers. As a result, many of its core consumers thought that the company had lost touch with what they really wanted and started shopping elsewhere, at chains such as Dollar General, Aldi, Inc., and Family Dollar. These "dollar store" retailers continued to nibble away at Wal-Mart's core shopper base, while a more aggressive Amazon began competing directly with Wal-Mart by offering even lower prices and the convenience of free delivery in many product lines. Many recession-pinched consumers felt that Wal-Mart no longer offered the best value for their hard-earned money.[34] A push into organic foods fizzled out, and Wal-Mart's remodeling of its stores tried to emphasize trendier items often at the expense of products that appealed to its traditional customer base. Likewise, customers grew increasingly aware that Wal-Mart's "rollback" pricing was very similar to the "high-low" pricing engaged by department stores and discount chains in the 1990s. A "low" price entices the customer to enter the store, only for him/her to find that most of the prices on the items that he/she wants are much "higher." Now, Wal-Mart has returned to its classic policy of low prices everyday, backed up by its tremendous economies of scale in purchasing and strong bargaining power with suppliers.[35]

Strategic Discipline: Operational Excellence

Central to all Consolidators' source of competitive advantage is the attainment of operational excellence in all of its activities. As a rule, Consolidators will devote most of their R&D spending toward process improvement, proprietary technologies, and skills in production and/or service operations. The search for newer and better ways to squeeze costs out of the system is their imperative. Reducing work-in-process, order fulfillment time, inventory holding costs, and supply chain complexity represent key priorities for Consolidators. Although improving product features remain important ways of attracting and retaining customers, Consolidators will devote more resources to making their offerings more consistent, reducing the number of steps to provide them, and striving for a low-cost leadership position in the marketplace, rather than spending resources on basic R&D activities. Emphasizing special, custom features or the latest breakthrough product designs are less important for Consolidators in their resource allocation designs. There are three critical ingredients of operational excellence for Consolidators:

1. cost efficiency;
2. continuous process refinement;
3. outsourcing.

Cost Efficiency

Consolidators seek cost reduction in every activity. Capturing and exploiting economies of scale in procurement, manufacturing, service provision, distribution, logistics, and service are critical for their cost-efficient platforms. Economies of scale are vital to lower the fixed unit costs that saddle Consolidators' large investments in their operational infrastructure. In some industries, such as groceries, fast food, and printing, Consolidators face such incredibly thin margins that the continuous streamlining of operations is necessary to sustain their low-cost advantage. This economic reality in turn drives Consolidators to identify and isolate all potential sources of costs—both tangible and latent. Tangible costs include all types of direct and indirect costs that the business incurs in providing the product or service that the customer purchases. A major tangible cost facing every firm is that of health care and employee benefits. To get a better grasp on its future spiraling health costs, Wal-Mart has signed up with six major health centers (Baylor, Scott & White) to provide heart and spinal surgeries to its employees and their families with no out-of-pocket costs. Wal-Mart's huge employee base enables the retailer to command enormous bargaining power, which has helped it to drive down its medical costs. Latent costs are much more difficult to identify and isolate. These include waste from excessively long order fulfillment times, excessive inventory stocks, underutilized plant and equipment, and skilled personnel performing unnecessary tasks. This is why so many large companies have undertaken internal cost improvement programs—for example, Six Sigma and Kaizen—to eliminate the hidden costs of inefficient operations.

One needs to look no further than Southwest Airlines for a model of cost-efficient operations built from the ground up from day one. Founded and led by CEO Herb Kelleher until his retirement in 2000, Southwest Airlines has consistently remained profitable in an industry dominated by too many airlines chasing too few passengers willing to pay premium fares. Southwest's low-cost operations underpin every activity, from aircraft procurement, to maintenance, to ground operations, and to serving customers. And despite its motto of fun and low fares, it has earned the undying loyalty of both its employees and customers.

To ensure low maintenance costs and fast-turnaround of aircraft repair, Southwest purchases only one type of aircraft, the Boeing 737, which is designed for the kind of short-haul flight in which Southwest dominates the market. Since workers are extremely familiar with the ins-and-outs of the 737 aircraft, they gain an exceptionally high level of expertise and proficiency working with it. This "experience effect" enables Southwest's maintenance crews to become ever more proficient at what they do, thus removing the kind of hidden and costly inefficiencies that plague larger airlines flying a variety of different aircraft models, each with their technical specifications. Maintenance activities have been located to Costa Rica, where costs are significantly lower than those in the United States.

Customers love the fast-turnaround of Southwest's flights. A typical Southwest plane spends no more than twenty minutes at a gate. With amazing speed, Southwest deplanes its passengers, unloads luggage, and then checks in a new group of passengers for the next flight. How does Southwest accomplish this efficiency each hour of every day? The company spends heavily to recruit the people who are most comfortable working in a cross-functional environment. Employees freely switch from one task to another as needed. Flight attendants help to clean the planes before each departure, and ticket agents also help reschedule passengers' itineraries when delays occur without the bureaucratic oversight and cumbersome procedures used at other carriers. Despite the company's cost-efficiency focus, Southwest seeks employees whom it believes will be people-oriented and innately cheerful.

Continuous Process Refinement

Consolidators that invest and manage their own large in-house operations must continue to refine their processes. Continuous improvement has remained a central theme in many companies' rising productivity, cost reduction, and increasing product quality. Consider the dominant cost leaders in the automotive industry (e.g., Toyota,

Hyundai), the steel industry (Posco of Korea, Baoshan of China), paints (DuPont, Valspar, Sherwin-Williams, the ICI unit of Akzo-Nobel, BASF), and Weyerhaeuser in the wood products and paper industries. All of these firms continue to uncover new and better ways of improving the productivity of their operations and their people. Refining the actual production or service provision process is also a must for Consolidators as it removes every possible source of variation that could negatively impact product quality or smooth operations. This was illustrated in our example of McDonald's approach to searching for the best possible French fry made with absolute consistency in every restaurant location.

The phrase "Intel Inside" denotes the fact that Intel-designed and manufactured microprocessors form the brains of many personal computers and other electronics devices. For the past 20 years, most people have equated "Intel Inside" with a marketing campaign to instill brand loyalty in a personal computer industry defined by "clones" that offer cut-rate features and pricing in their imitation of Hewlett-Packard, Dell, and IBM. However, the other side of "Intel Inside" speaks of a corporate-wide obsession with learning, applying, and standardizing the best practices possible to ensure perfect micro-processor quality. Within each of Intel's "Chipzilla" plants (each of which costs upward of $5 billion or more to build), the layout of the "fab" is exactly the same, right down to the color and position of the floor tiles. Each stage of the chip manufacturing and fabrication process follows a precise formula for equipment location to ensure that costly work-in-process and unbalanced process flows are totally eliminated. Despite the gargantuan cost of each "fab," Intel believes that its long experience with manufacturing process refinement endows it with a major sustainable advantage of its competitors that have shifted to higher degrees of outsourcing in recent years.

A focus on continuous process refinement is by no means limited to high-tech capital-intensive businesses. At QuikTrip, for example, a convenience store chain with more than 540 U.S. stores and $8 billion in sales, a deep understanding of how to design efficient but eye-pleasing and clean service stations in which customers can be served quickly has enabled this private company to capture significant profitability in an industry driven almost entirely by low gasoline prices. Employees are cross-functionally trained to perform a variety of tasks from checking out customers to brewing coffee to doing janitorial work. Logistical processes, including everything from merchandise ordering to moving merchandise around in the store, are timed and standardized across all stores to maximize freshness and convenience. Employees are empowered to decide how many units of each product item to order, and automated inventory replenishment and paperless payments are then used to execute these transactions. QuikTrip believes that empowering employees in these ways makes them responsive to local needs and preferences, as well as increasing customer and employee satisfaction. By standardizing processes, employees also can move from store to store since all have the same design.

Matching process design with employee training and skills provides the foundation for QuikTrip's competitive advantage. CEO Chet Cadieux believes that extroverted employees sell more—and like each other more—than introverted people. QuikTrip hires extroverted people because they are more likely to engage the customer with small talk, and small talk increases customer satisfaction. Once hired, all full-time employees receive two weeks of training and part-timers receive 40 hours. During this training, QuikTrip's management explains how employees contribute to the firm's exceptional focus on key tasks rooted in its operations-driven discipline. For example, employees quickly learn that they need to open up cash registers as soon as lines build at the check-out counter. Likewise, employees are expected to clean the inside and outside of the service station to exacting standards, ensuring that trash does not fill up in disposal bins, automated gas dispensers have paper to process credit-card transactions, and windshield cleaning fluids remain filled for customers' convenience. Inside the QT station, employees also are taught to monitor how long food is cooked and warmed to ensure freshness and even preparation. The end result: this tight connection between a superbly-designed retail process and cross-trained employees has just a 13 per cent turnover rate among employees, compared to a 59 per cent industry average, and 66 per cent higher sales per hour than other convenience stores.

Outsourcing

Consolidators across many industries have steadily relied on outsourcing to further reduce costs. Some companies have developed very strong competitive advantages through business models that revolved around "asset-light" operations. Witness the enormous success Cisco Systems has enjoyed. It is the standard-bearer and market share leader of almost all types of telecommunications and networking equipment. Central to Cisco's enormous success has been its two-pronged strategy to grow via acquisition of smaller, Pioneer companies possessing a key breakthrough technology, and a well-developed set of supplier relationships in which its manufacturing partners do all of the work of building Cisco's gear. Some of Cisco's most important partners are the contract electronics manufacturers (CEMs) that take the larger company's product designs and transform them into tangible items. These CEMs in turn deliver Cisco-branded products directly to Cisco's corporate, telecom, and networking customers regardless of location. Over the years, Cisco has relied heavily on the Taiwan Semiconductor Manufacturing Company (TSMC) to build custom-designed chips; CEMs such as Solectron and Flextronics, to build the bridges, routers, and hubs that form the Internet's "plumbing"; and a host of transportation/logistics companies to deliver the product straight to the customer.

Outsourcing has become common even among many service-oriented businesses as well, as US Airways and CVS-Caremark demonstrate. U.S.-based airlines have increasingly outsourced the maintenance of their aircraft fleets to less costly locations around the world, including Canada, Singapore, Mexico, and China. For example, outsourcing of airline maintenance resulted in cost reductions of 31 per cent to US Airways and 23 per cent to United.[36]

Consider the increasing reliance in the United States of managed care firms and large employers on pharmacy-benefit managers (PBMs) to handle the growing array of retail-provided and mail-order prescription drugs covered under employee benefit plans. PBMs include companies such as Amerisource-Bergen, Cardinal Health, the Caremark unit of CVS-Caremark, and the biggest one of all, ExpressScripts. PBMs have invested heavily in cutting-edge inventory management systems and advanced database systems to coordinate the patient needs for prescription drugs with employee-benefit plans and managed care firms that administer drug costs. As managed care firms continue their industry-wide consolidation efforts, the pharmacy-benefit managers have also followed suit. In 2012, Medco Containment merged with ExpressScripts to form one of the largest PBM companies in the U.S. This combined entity will probably have enormous influence over the pricing of many prescription drugs sold at drug stores or delivered directly to the customer's home.

Strategic Dangers for Consolidators

Consolidators face inherent risks emanating from their search for cost efficiency, large size, and focus on process refinement. Although today's Consolidators may enjoy large market shares, they are prone to three critical dangers:

1. the boiling frog syndrome;
2. increasing irrelevance in the industry;
3. dilution of core business.

The strategic vulnerabilities of Consolidators are portrayed in Table 6.6.

Let's examine the organizational and managerial implications of each danger.

Table 6.6 Perils of Consolidators
• Avoid "groupthink" in decision-making
• Do not let process excellence focus mean ignoring the customers' shifting needs
• Do not compromise product quality in zeal to cut costs

The Boiling Frog Syndrome

The term "boiling frog" was coined by former GE CEO Jack Welch, who explained the underlying dynamics of how large organizations eventually get into trouble. He once said that if you threw a frog into pot of boiling water, the frog would instinctively leap out and thus save itself. However, if you put the same frog into a pot of water that slowly and steadily boils over time, the frog eventually becomes comfortable sitting in the pot (since it feels like a sauna) and is eventually lulled into a slow death.

Consolidators are prone to the "boiling frog syndrome" largely because of their size, organizational structures, and reward systems. They tend to overvalue "groupthink" and top-down directives at the expense of experimentation, risk-taking, and creativity. While the Consolidator's most important strategic imperatives revolve around attaining cost efficiencies and process refinement, pursuit of these goals can undermine the Consolidator's awareness of important shifts in the marketplace, changing customer needs, and the rise of new technologies/competitors that can render the Consolidator's fixed costs investments and methodologies obsolete.

Consolidators that have built up large market shares over time may be seduced into believing that their business processes and strategic approaches are invulnerable to new external developments. Over time, managers in Consolidators are likely to develop something that management researchers have termed a "dominant logic," which refers to a "mental map" or cognitive reference frame as to what is best for the business. A Consolidator's success in capturing ever greater cost efficiencies and process improvements forms the basis for beliefs, expectations, norms, and priorities about what the business should do. In turn, these attributes reinforce the existing organizational structure, systems, processes, and reward systems. When the business continues to prosper, the dominant logic becomes further ingrained in the organization's DNA. When the organization faces a major change in its external environment, the pre-existing dominant logic can impede the Consolidator's managers from understanding the new competitive, customer, and technological realities impacting the business.

Ironically, the most recent pervasive evidence a long-held "dominant logic" contributing to a massive "boiling frog syndrome" can be found deep in the heart of corporate Japan. Panasonic, Hitachi, Sony, Sharp, Toshiba, and Mitsubishi face the reality that they have completely missed the boat in terms of designing consumer electronics products for the mass market. All of these Japanese giants flourished throughout from the 1970s right through to the 1990s by producing innovative products such as the Sony Walkman, Sharp Aquos television sets, LCD screens, sleek home stereo systems, and advanced semiconductors and laser devices. As Japanese firms steamrollered their U.S. and European competitors, the "dominant logic" of keeping all manufacturing in-house, promoting engineers above all other functions to key leadership positions, and remaining tone-deaf to customers' needs, especially in foreign markets, became ever more deeply embedded. In addition, the time-honored Japanese practice of "nemawashi," or root-building, severely constrained the firm's ability to act quickly. "Nemawashi" is an informal process of quietly laying the foundation to assess some proposed change by talking to concerned parties and gathering support and feedback for the status quo. It is a key to consensus decision-making that effectively stymied creative debate internally. Yet, these same giants are now stumbling badly, having missed the rise of Apple's iPod, iPhone, and iPad appliances, and have lost market share to Samsung. Despite the many signs of changing consumer tastes, Japanese firms acted as if nothing really changed. Costs ballooned as the Japanese yen steadily appreciated, but companies decided not to outsource anything—even the most mundane and basic parts or subassemblies. Only last year did Hitachi announce that it would outsource all television production, a business in which it had been losing money for almost a decade. Toshiba's CEO even acknowledged that his firm, along with rivals, has been particularly late in taking drastic steps to restructure and realign operations. Yet, he still acknowledges that his management teams remain unable to predict market trends.[37]

The retailing industry offers numerous other lessons to managers about the great dangers of the "boiling frog syndrome." Consider the slow "death-by-a-thousand-cuts" of retailing icon K-Mart that occurred for most of the past three decades. Perhaps best known for its "Blue

Light Specials," in which the store would periodically offer a deep discount in one section of the store throughout the day, K-Mart became a retailing powerhouse for much of the 1970s. During the 1980s, however, senior management allowed its stores to decay and customer service deteriorated. Even worse, K-Mart did not invest in some of the newer technologies that would have facilitated a more efficient inventory management system and a continuously replenished supply chain to ensure that stores had the requisite amount of merchandise as advertised in its newspaper fliers. At the same time that K-Mart's inertia deepened, Wal-Mart began to expand from its southern U.S. roots to blanket the entire country. Using the latest computerized technologies that could provide instantaneous information about any store's inventory, daily purchasing patterns, and perpetual replenishment, Wal-Mart became the overwhelming dominant force in retailing as K-Mart sank into bankruptcy and its eventual purchase by Sears Holdings. The length of time that it takes a company to "boil" depends on its financial resources and the dynamics of the industry in which it competes.

The "boiling frog syndrome" represents a major potential danger zone for all Consolidators. Once a Consolidator has fallen prey to it, it is extremely difficult to reverse without an extreme crisis or major catastrophe. Often, Consolidators face the growing risk of becoming increasingly obsolete as their core markets shift, or more importantly, the underlying technology defining their offerings fundamentally changes or "disrupts" the business. Thus, Consolidators facing the specter of such massively "disruptive" change will need to become Reinventors that need to "unlearn" all of their organizational practices in order to learn new sources of competitive advantage in the future (see Chapter 7). Those Consolidators that do not see the need to Reinvent themselves ultimately face growing irrelevance in the industry.

Increasing Irrelevance in the Industry

Consolidators that remain stuck in their ways eventually face a steady erosion of their market share as customers flock elsewhere to purchase a more competitive offering, or their key product/service itself becomes irrelevant to today's needs. Consider the enormous travails faced by two high-flying giants in their respective arenas: RadioShack and Sears in retailing; as well as Research in Motion, Ltd. (known for its BlackBerry communication devices) and Nokia, a former giant of the world markets for cellular phones.

RadioShack and Sears used to be legends of U.S. retailing. RadioShack's decade-long effort to reposition itself now faces a liquidity crunch that threatens to catapult the 91-year-old company into bankruptcy. Primarily located in strip malls throughout the United States RadioShack never understood the depth of its decline as consumers increasingly turned to the Internet to order electronics, cameras, telephones, and other gadgets. Once synonymous with selling electronic components and parts, RadioShack has seen its customer base moving away from fixing their own analog electronics products to purchasing all types of digital products that are not worth repairing. Over the past ten years, RadioShack attempted to recast itself as a seller of digital phones, only to be again crushed by the cell-phone providers (e.g., AT&T, Verizon Wireless, Sprint) offering phones through their own stores. Now, the company still labors under the image of offering nothing relevant to today's customers' needs.[38]

Similarly, Sears Holdings (the owner of both Sears and now K-Mart) has begun closing over 1,200 stores to raise cash over the next few years. Many retailing analysts state that this is the final "death spiral" for Sears as it seeks a way to eventually exit from all of its retail operations. Although current CEO Ed Lampert hopes to restore Sears' luster through the selective introduction of new retailing technologies, Sears has lost consumers' confidence. Unlike many retailers that rent space in malls, Sears owns the majority of its stores. These stores, in turn, require significant expenditures for upkeep and periodic remodeling. Consumers have remarked that many Sears stores seem outdated and grittier than in the past as management seeks to further control cash outflows. Even though it possesses several popular brands such as Kenmore appliances and Craftsman tools, consumers increasingly purchase these items elsewhere, often online or at other competitors like Best Buy. Sears has already shuttered its Great Outdoors unit, which sold higher-end appliances and home furnishings to well-heeled consumers.[39]

The stunningly fast decline of Research in Motion (RIM) over the past ten years stems from many factors. Perhaps the most important was senior management's fervent belief that the BlackBerry's proprietary design, operating system, and secure transmission network would shield the company from encroaching new technologies and rivals, such as Apple, Samsung, Google's Android operating system, and HTC. Founded in 1984, RIM pioneered the idea of e-mail on the move. At its zenith market valuation in 2008, RIM was worth over $80 billion, but as of June 2012 had plunged to $5 billion. RIM executives thought that the easy-to-use keyboard for e-mail would rank highest in customers' priorities, especially for busy people who increasingly communicate via text messages and short e-mail bursts while on the move. When Apple introduced its iPhone in 2007, few RIM executives saw the threat. They were convinced that BlackBerry users would never relinquish their small keyboard-based devices for the capacitive, OLED touch screens that define the iPhone's exceptional versatility, sleekness, and fashion-like statement. Managers, employees, and consumers increasingly brought their iPhones to work, and began using them for business purposes over their employers' wireless networks rather than relying on RIM's in-house transmission network, despite its superior security features. In effect, RIM lost a series of opportunities to design a new type of smartphone that incorporated an increasing number of computer-like functions and applications (apps). What complicated RIM's "boiling frog" quandary was a growing split between two key factions in the C-suite: one wanted to accelerate in-house product development of new tablets that could compete with Apple, while another wanted to license BlackBerry's network to other telecom companies to expand the reach of its market penetration. Currently, RIM has attempted to introduce a new type of iPhone-like device known as the Z-10 that will offer the same type of touch-screen technology commonly found on Apple and Android devices. However, the Z-10 met with a chilly reception in February 2013 as CEO Thorsten Heins announced that production delays had slowed the phone's availability for the U.S. market. These delays also mean that corporate customers will likely accelerate their migration to other Apple or Android phone platforms, thus potentially causing RIM even greater loss of market share. A lack of sufficient "apps" to interest potential buyers will probably exacerbate the situation.[40]

In a related vein, Finnish telecommunications giant Nokia was synonymous with designing the hippest, coolest-looking phones throughout the 1990s. Having a Nokia was a fashion statement akin to wearing Adidas or Nike. Nokia rose to pre-eminence around 1996 when it became one of the first cell phone makers to offer a digital wireless phone to the mass market. Ironically, Nokia beat Motorola to the market because Motorola believed that its robust and sturdy analog-based handsets would remain the leading industry technology—something it helped to introduce in the mid-1980s. Nokia vaulted into the elite of cutting-edge technology companies with successive waves of boldly designed digital phones that incorporated an ever-expanding array of features, such as MP3 music players, digital cameras, text messaging, rudimentary e-mail, and even online gaming. Its Communicator-branded line of phones became the "must-have" gadgets for millions around the world, and its global factories kept churning out the latest desired products. At one point, the world's largest manufacturer of digital cameras was not Nikon, Olympus, Casio, Canon, or Fuji, but Nokia! However, the company began to struggle as customers migrated to smartphones that came with advanced web-driven software, customized "apps," and sleeker touchscreen features. As with RIM, Nokia has lost much of its momentum after Apple introduced its iPhone, and the company now faces a multitude of competitors, including smartphones powered by Android and even Windows-based software phones made by Taiwan's HTC.

To resuscitate its moribund business, Nokia has now partnered ever more closely with Microsoft in a bet that the Windows 8 operating system will become a viable competitor to Apple and Google. Yet, Nokia continues to suffer from significant product development delays, as long decision-making times and a clannish corporate culture limit fast responses to fickle customers and swiftly changing market conditions. Nokia also relied heavily on its own proprietary Symbian operating system for a long time, hoping that it would enable it to carve out a dominant share of the market. However, the operating system proved difficult to upgrade and frustrated customers who wanted a truly fast and agile cell phone. Unfortunately for both Nokia and its partner Microsoft, both companies are now lagging far behind Apple and Google not only in terms of market acceptance and penetration, but also in the number of "apps" written for use on the Windows-based operating system.[41]

Dilution of Core Business

It is only natural for Consolidators to search for new business opportunities in order to sustain their profitability. As Consolidators face the unrelenting pressures of industry maturity, diversifying into new arenas becomes an extremely appealing vehicle to escape the merciless price wars and furious fights to retain market share. When Consolidators *do* attempt to diversify into new markets to escape their current arenas, however, they can run into another set of dangers—that of diluting and undermining their core business.

Many analysts believe that PepsiCo is now facing the aftershocks of having taken its eye off the ball when managing its core beverage business. Under CEO Indra Nooyi, PepsiCo undertook a major effort to create and promote a line of "Good for You" foods that pushed the company into health foods since she became CEO in 2006. Although it remains a major force in beverages and snack foods (via its Frito-Lay unit), over the past six years PepsiCo began to acquire yogurt and grain-enriched dairy food companies. At one point, the company hoped to more than double its annual revenues from nutrition and health food products to $30 billion by 2020.[42] This expensive push into these new arenas came with a major price tag: advertising budgets for its traditional Pepsi line of beverages were diverted to these new businesses. Moreover, Frito-Lay's snack food business faced rising commodity costs for corn and packaged materials, while PepsiCo's Tropicana orange unit started to lose market share to archrival Coke's Simply Juice brand. Pepsi's Gatorade also faces slow market share declines. Spending prodigiously on health food products came at a huge cost.[43] At one point, the flagship Pepsi brand trailed behind not only Coke, but Diet Coke as well. To revive these products, PepsiCo's management attempted to redesign the packaging and to remake Tropicana with a new juice bottle format. However, these marketing missteps cost the company valuable time. Pepsi also skipped advertising its soda on the 2010 Super Bowl for the first time in over 24 years, and instead devoted those funds to charity competitions that did little to sell more beverages. Although CEO Nooyi fervently believes that PepsiCo's customers will still want healthier products, it is not clear that Pepsi can catch up with such established giants such as Danone and Nestlé, who have been in this business for a much longer time.[44]

In 2012, however, PepsiCo recommitted itself to promoting its existing line of beverages, especially sodas. Advertising budgets were increased by as much as $600 million for 2012 and a corporate-wide reorganization aimed to recapture the marketing magic that once made Pepsi's ads among some of the most memorable. Regional marketing offices were consolidated to strengthen the beverage business' leverage with its retail buyers. A renewed marketing emphasis on Pepsi, Mountain Dew, Gatorade, Tropicana, and Lipton spearheaded the company's return to its core business.[45]

Not all attempts to rejuvenate or to revitalize Consolidators' businesses are necessarily fraught with extreme dangers. IBM, for example, has undergone a 20-year transition that has seen it recapture its lead and reputation as one of the world's premier technology companies. Although the company has long been a powerful innovator and provider of state-of-the-art technologies across a broad spectrum of businesses (e.g., computer hardware, semiconductors, software, systems integration, database management, middleware), it too has faced major questions of how best to deal with industry maturity impacting its most important core businesses. For example, in 1993, IBM lost much of its magic when Intel and Microsoft seized the lead in personal computers. IBM also fell behind Cisco Systems when it came to networking technologies that laid the "plumbing" of the Internet. Even worse, its core mainframe business was on the way to losing billions of dollars annually as corporate customers switched to lower-cost platforms from other firms, and newer types of technologies that could provide many of the computing features of large mainframe computers, but at a fraction of the cost and maintenance. Under former CEOs Lou Gerstner and Sam Palmisano, IBM restored its focus on innovating new products that complemented its core mainframe expertise. Instead of looking at the mainframe business as a candidate for divestiture, IBM's management decided to show the power of its computers when it introduced Deep Blue, an advanced supercomputer that beat legendary chess champion Gary Kasparov in a worldwide televised tournament in 1997. Under both Gerstner and Palmisano, IBM continued to invest in new lines of business that complemented its existing hardware and software strengths, with a special focus on "data analytics."[46] Data analytics (or "big data" in industry parlance) is the use of high-powered software to search for ever more intricate patterns that are almost impossible to detect when examining billion upon billions of data points. They can be used to capture what customers are likely to buy at any given moment based on knowledge of their prior purchase patterns. Big data represents a huge business opportunity for IBM as it develops ever more powerful computing platforms, advanced software, and consulting services that will help large corporate customers, health-care organizations, and governments looking to research new ways of understanding day-to-day phenomenon that are currently inexplicable through conventional technologies. CEO Palmisano even launched IBM into a new vision of creating a "Smarter Planet," where pollution, traffic, weather systems, and even online shopping can be tracked to predict potential future patterns that will help businesses save costs and avoid major risks.[47]

German giant Siemens is also in the midst of a major transition that seeks to take this huge provider of lighting, machinery, medical equipment, locomotives, and advanced factory systems into new lines of businesses. Under CEO Peter Löscher, Siemens has sharpened its focus on what it believes will be its future core businesses. Siemens has always been known for its enormous prowess in research, cutting-edge products, and a rich supply of product ideas in its development pipelines. The company has sometimes suffered from being slow to respond to the marketplace, however, and in many instances, time-to-market has taken second place to technical excellence. While this has awarded Siemens with a well-deserved reputation for top-notch quality, the company had often experienced difficulty allocating resources to those businesses with the greatest promise. Under CEO Löscher,

Siemens has re-energized itself by exiting from its slow-growth telecom business, once a crown jewel. Löscher has also shut down its computer businesses, believing that they were much too small to compete effectively. Löscher, a GE alumnus, is beginning to transform Siemens in much the same way that Jack Welch did at GE when he became CEO in 1980. Both CEOs believed in instilling tight cost controls and financial discipline to ensure that resources are allocated to the projects with the biggest overall return to their businesses. Fast execution has become the mantra at the new Siemens, where Löscher is now introducing much more stringent accountability at each business unit. Siemens continues to streamline and exit from its smaller business positions, while C-level managers are now asked to cooperate more frequently as the divisional fiefdoms lose their once-protected silos.[48]

MASTERING THE ESSENTIALS OF A CONSOLIDATOR

Mastering the essentials of a consolidator involves:

- keeping a laser-like focus on cost efficiency in everything the firm does;
- investing in new methods and techniques to undertake continuous process improvement;
- outsourcing activities that further enhance cost efficiency;
- ensuring that products meet customer needs without compromising quality;
- leveraging the firm's bargaining power with its suppliers and buyers to capture even greater economies of scale in procurement and sales;

and avoiding the following:

- assuming that large size means the firm does not have to change as its customers do;
- compromising product quality to achieve short-term cost savings;
- believing that consensus is synonymous with an effective decision.

Notes

1 A thorough exposition of industry maturity can be found in Michael E. Porter, *Competitive Advantage*, Free Press, New York, 1985.

2 See R. L. Katz, M. E. Weise, and D. H. Yang, "Consolidation: The Wireless Way," *Strategy + Business*, Volume 29, 2002, pp. 46–53.

3 See "WellPoint to Buy 1–800-Contacts," *Wall Street Journal*, June 4, 2012, p. B3.

4 See R. Goldberg and C. Knoop, "ConAgra: Across the Food Chain," Harvard Business School Case, Number 9–999-010, Boston, MA, Harvard Business School Publishing, 1999.

5 See "The New GE Way: Go Deep, Not Wide," *Wall Street Journal*, March 7, 2012, pp. B1, B9.

6 See "How Japan's Sharp Lost Its Edge," *Wall Street Journal*, March 20, 2012, p. B3; also "Toshiba's Chief Takes Stock," *Wall Street Journal*, April 10, 2012, p. B8.

7 "For AMR, a Vast New Network," *Wall Street Journal*, February 8, 2013, pp. B1, B2.

8 See "Febreze Joins P&G's $1 Billion Club," *Wall Street Journal*, March 9, 2011, p. B7.

9 See "As Middle Class Shrinks, P&G Aims High and Low," *Wall Street Journal*, September 12, 2011, pp. A1, A16.

10 See "P&G Sheds Pringles," *Wall Street Journal*, April 6, 2011, p. B4; also, "P&G Realigns Main Units As a Top Executive Retires," *Wall Street Journal*, February 2, 2011, p. B3.

11 See "At P&G, Beauty Makeover Needs to Prove It Has Legs," *Wall Street Journal*, January 26, 2011, pp. B1, B7. Also see "P&G Gets a Lift From Price Cuts," *Wall Street Journal*, August 4–5, 2012, p. B4.

12 See "Foxconn Buys Into Sharp," *Wall Street Journal*, March 28, 2012, pp. B1, B4. Also see "Hon Hai-Sharp Alliance Shows Sign of Fraying," *Wall Street Journal*, August 4–5, 2012, p. B3.

13 See "Yum's CEO Serves Up New Taco, Growth Plans," *Wall Street Journal*, February 21, 2012, p. B7.

14 See "Micron to Acquire Japanese Rival Elpida," *Wall Street Journal*, July 3, 2012, p. B3.

15 See "Apple-Amazon War Heats Up," *Wall Street Journal*, July 26, 2012, p. B3.

16 See "Amazon's Margins Improve," *Wall Street Journal*, January 29, 2013, p. B1.

17 See "Amazon to Challenge iPad," *Wall Street Journal*, September 26, 2011, p. B6.

18 See "Amazon Fights the iPad With 'Fire'," *Wall Street Journal*, September 29, 2011, pp. B1, B10.

19 See "Magazines Join With New Tablet Challenger," *Wall Street Journal*, September 29, 2011, pp. B1, B10.

20 See "Kindle Catches Fire," *Wall Street Journal*, November 29, 2011, p. B6.

21 See "CEO of the Internet," *Wired*, December 2011, pp. 200–215, 244–245.

22 See "Amazon Goes After Netflix, Adding Movie Subscription," *Wall Street Journal*, February 23, 2011, pp. B1, B4.

23 See "Amazon vs. Netflix: Streaming Battle Heats Up," *Wall Street Journal*, February 1, 2013, p. B1.

24 See "Amazon Adds That Robotic Touch," *Wall Street Journal*, March 20, 2012, pp. B1, B6.

25 See "Logical Step: Samsung Shifts Its Focus for Chips," *Wall Street Journal*, January 26, 2012, p. B4.

26 See "HTC Investors Head for Exits," *Wall Street Journal*, August 8, 2012, pp. B1, B2.

27 See "The Two-Horse Smartphone Race," *Wall Street Journal*, April 24, 2012, pp. B1, B4.

28 Ibid.; also see "How Samsung Turned Up the Sizzle," *Fortune*, July 25, 2011, p. 28.

29 See "Samsung Moves to Boost Software," *Wall Street Journal*, September 21, 2011, p. B6.

30 See "Super Style Me," *Fast Company*, October 2010, pp. 104–112.

31 See "How McDonald's Hit the Hot Spot," *Wall Street Journal*, December 13, 2011, pp. B1, B2.

32 Carl Sewell, *Customers for Life*, Crown Business, Random House, New York, 2002, p. 25.

33 Andrew Grove, *Only the Paranoid Survive*, Profile Books, 1998.

34 See "Wal-Mart Loses Edge," *Wall Street Journal*, August 16, 2011, pp. B1, B2.

35 See "Wal-Mart Tries to Recapture Mr. Sam's Winning Formula," *Wall Street Journal*, February 22, 2011, pp. A1, A12.

36 See "American Airlines May Outsource More Maintenance," *Fort Worth Star-Telegram*, February 4, 2012.

37 See "Toshiba's Chief Takes Stock," *Wall Street Journal*, April 10, 2012, p. B8; also, "A Long Road Ahead for Japan Tech Giants," *Wall Street Journal*, August 2, 2010, p. B6.

38 See "RadioShack Still Suffers from Old-Fashioned Image," *Wall Street Journal*, July 26, 2012, p. B3.

39 See "In Retreat, Sears Set to Unload Stores," *Wall Street Journal*, February 24, 2012, pp. B1, B2.

40 See "Prospects Dim for BlackBerry Maker," *Wall Street Journal*, May 30, 2012, pp. B1, B2; also "Multiple Missteps Led to RIM's Fall," *Wall Street Journal*, June 28, 2012, pp. A1, A14; "Has RIM Lost Its Core," *Wall Street Journal*, January 29, 2013, pp. B1, B2; "Finally, a BlackBerry—But More Delays," *Wall Street Journal*, January 31, 2013, pp. B1, B4.

41 See "Missed Call: Nokia Reversal of Fortune is Also Finland's," *Wall Street Journal*, June 3, 2011, p. A12; also "Nokia Shows Off New Phones," *Wall Street Journal*, June 22, 2011, p. B6; "It's Crunch Time for Nokia," *Wall Street Journal*, October 25, 2011, p. B6.

42 See "PepsiCo Shakes Up Management," *Wall Street Journal*, September 15, 2011, p. B3.

43 See "PepsiCo Board Stands by Nooyi," *Wall Street Journal*, January 13, 2012, pp. B1, B2.

44 See "PepsiCo Wakes Up and Smells the Cola," *Wall Street Journal*, June 28, 2011, pp. B1, B2.

45 See "PepsiCo Overhauls Strategy," *Wall Street Journal*, February 10, 2012, p. B3.

46 See "IBM Ready for Close-Up," *Wall Street Journal*, January 18, 2011, p. B4.

47 See "IBM's Super Second Act," *Fortune*, March 21, 2011, pp. 115–124.

48 See "How Siemens Got Its Geist Back," *Business Week*, January 31, 2011, pp. 18–20.

7

REINVENTORS

Former Intel CEO Andy Grove once wrote that every firm in every industry will face a crisis point that determines whether it survives. Grove describes this crisis as an "inflection point." It forces senior management to take drastic action to change how their business thinks, operates, and competes for the future. In practice, this "inflection point" can spring forth from any number of sources: a fundamental technological breakthrough or change that renders the business' products/ services obsolete; a change in the regulatory landscape that breaks down barriers to entry and/or reconfigures the industry landscape; a totally new way that customers perceive or derive value from their purchases; or the arrival of a new type of competitor that changes the rules of industry competition. Grove noted that Intel faced an inflection point of massive proportions when Japanese semiconductor firms essentially drove down memory prices in the mid-1980s to such an extent that Intel decided to exit the memory business that it had helped pioneer and lead for nearly two decades. Under no illusion that the Japanese onslaught would end anytime soon, Intel refocused its efforts to become the dominant microprocessor producer in the world.[1]

At some point, then, every business will face a defining moment. Doing business as usual will no longer be the source of its competitive advantage. Instead, the same business that delivered profitability and competitive success time after time becomes an albatross that hinders a company's ability to compete in the future. When a pre-existing business begins to hinder a firm's ability to compete, it must *reinvent* itself to survive.

Leading management theorist Clayton Christensen has written extensively on the notion of "disruptive technologies" that lay the foundation for "disruptive innovation." In a spirit similar to that of Grove, Christensen notes that "disruptive innovations" rewrite the rules of competition along a number of important dimensions:

- How does the business re-organize itself to learn and develop the new skills necessary to embrace the "disruption"?
- How does the business reconfigure and redesign its value-adding processes to take advantage of the "disruption"?
- How does the business go about offering new value propositions to its customers?

Christensen notes that every firm facing the onslaught of disruptive technologies and innovations will have to confront life-and-death questions about its survival: What new core competencies must it learn, how must it prioritize resource allocation to new product development, and what kind of organization design will best suit the impacted business?[2]

Reinventors are typically large businesses, many of which are part of multi-product diversified firms, or even conglomerates. Some of these products compete in a mature industry that is at the epicenter of a massive change in the way value is created, produced, and delivered to the customer. Most often, Reinventors will face technological break-throughs that completely redefine how a product/service is created, or how a customer uses its product/service. As an existing product line becomes obsolete, the decline in market share will ideally spur a company's efforts to reinvent itself. In practice, however, reinvention efforts are enormously difficult and complex endeavors. Firms do not willingly "unlearn" their core competencies. Businesses that do not learn the new core competencies and methods to reinvent themselves will soon become irrelevant and die, as did Eastman Kodak, Blockbuster, and

Borders. On the other hand, full-service brokerages, such as Merrill Lynch and UBS Paine Webber, completely revamped and redesigned their business models in the late 1990s (after much angst) to successfully deal with the exponentially rising popularity of online brokerages that offered the convenience of fast trading at much lower prices.

The challenge of adapting to disruptive technological change looms large over well-established businesses, but it is not the sole impetus for reinvention. Other environmental developments—for example, a major change in government regulations or the arrival of a completely new type of competitor—can also trigger the need for reinvention. Regulatory changes can alter the industry landscape by raising or lowering the barriers to entry, and thereby eroding long-protected profit sanctuaries. In the pharmaceutical industry, for example, changes in patent regulation or in the way courts interpret patents can dramatically impact the expected long-term profitability of a drug that took decades to develop, test, and commercialize, just as the advent of a new type of breakthrough treatment regimen might. Similarly, the advent of the U.S. Affordable Care Act of 2010 promises to redefine how health insurance firms, such as Cigna, Aetna, and WellPoint, will offer new health-care plans to customers as government-influenced price controls begin to set in. In a different vein, the arrival of a completely new type of competitor into an industry can force businesses into reinvention mode. For example, many colleges and universities today now face a new type of competitor that may ultimately impact their curriculum and pricing—for-profit universities are promising to educate new students by using virtual, distance-based learning in order to create customized education programs. Figure 7.1 portrays the critical strategic and organizational attributes of Reinventors.

Triggers for Reinvention

The "inflection points" that can buffet any industry are often unexpected. What makes reinvention such an urgent matter is that in many cases, the firm does not detect or sense the looming danger to their business and their sources of competitive advantage until much later. Early erosion of market share suddenly takes on a nosedive; customers defect

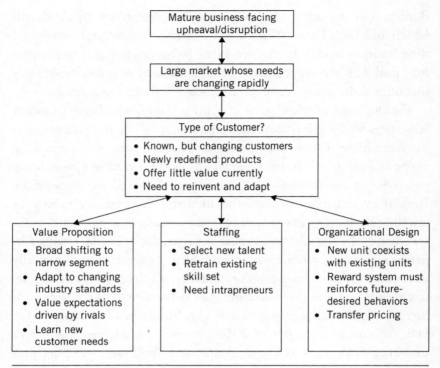

Figure 7.1 The Foundation of a Reinventor.

and begin to use breakthrough products or services differently; and the firm's cost position somehow now seems to be out of whack. Senior management either is unaware of the shifting sands, or is unable to gauge their impact on the firm's business model. In our discussion, the primary triggers for reinvention are the following:

- the advent of a "disruptive technology";
- regulatory change in an industry;
- the unforeseen arrival of a new type of competitor.

Advent of a Disruptive Technology

Simply put, a disruptive technology redefines how value is created, produced, and delivered in an industry. The most potent disruptive technologies rapidly undermine a firm's business model to such an extent that the core product itself is rendered completely obsolete and irrelevant. Consider the following examples of products that have disappeared over the past few decades:

- video-cassette recorders;
- compact discs for recorded music;
- pagers;
- pay phones;
- glass syringes;
- dedicated word-processing workstations;
- carburetors in vehicles.

In all these cases, a completely new way of creating and delivering value displaced the pre-existing product. Digital wireless technologies have completely displaced the need for pagers, payphones, and even voice mail today; plastic syringes make it so much easier to safely deliver drugs at a fraction of the cost (and risk of breakage) of traditional glass syringes; and word-processing software has even become freely available over the Internet.

Now, let's examine some industries where disruptive technologies are already transforming how we receive value today:

- e-readers and e-books;
- online education;
- 3-D printing;
- robotic surgical techniques;
- digital patient records;
- custom drug delivery methods;
- nanotechnology;
- data analytics (or "big data").

Why does all this matter? Disruptive technologies can emanate from any industry and impact any product or service. For many industries, the pace of technology change is likely to accelerate, and disruptive impacts will become more frequent. This means that every business will at some point face some type of disruption. The growth of the Internet, for example, is one such phenomenon that has already created, transformed, and decimated thousands of businesses over the past 20 years. Witness the decline of all kinds of brick-and-mortar businesses that were unable to reinvent themselves to take advantage of it: travel agencies, retailers, video rental outlets, and even banking. Even firms that led the way in creating new advertising media over the past decade now face disruption from the likes of Facebook, Google, and Twitter. What are the common themes underlying a disruptive technology? They fundamentally rewrite competition along three critical dimensions:

1.   how value is created;
2.   how the customer perceives and prices the new source of value;
3.   what skills, knowledge, and technology define the business' future.

Reinventors must question everything they do on each of these three dimensions.

Value Creation
The common thread of disruptive technologies is that they transform how a product or service is designed, produced, and delivered. In most cases, a disruptive technology eliminates one or more costly or time-consuming steps in the value-creation process, or completely changes the nature of the design, ingredient, component, or method that is at the heart of value creation. When disruptive technology creates a new avenue for creating value, it simultaneously destroys the economic underpinning of pre-existing avenues. Businesses must completely rethink how they will learn to compete in these new avenues. They must ask themselves hard questions about what to do with current production facilities and supply chain relationships. Reinventors must ask whether they even possess the necessary resources and skills to step up to the next level. For example, e-books and e-readers completely eliminate the need for producing print books and the associated presses that once defined a publishing house's core competence. Major textbook

publishers, such as Cengage, Palgrave Macmillan, and Houghton Harcourt Mifflin, are in the midst of major convulsive changes in the wake of new e-book production technology. Houghton is contending with bankruptcy proceedings as it seeks to reorganize and grapple with technology's impact on future textbook sales. Around the world, people are now reading e-books in planes, in parks, and in the doctor's office via their Kindles, Galaxies, iPads, Nooks, and smartphones. Barnes & Noble, for example, now faces critical questions about how to reinvent itself in the wake of how people are choosing to purchase and read. In other industries, we have seen how filmless cameras that use new types of microchips eliminate the need for film. And of course, the rise of Internet-enabled technologies has changed the way music is packaged and delivered to customers. CDs, pioneered in 1982, have now become a thing of the past.

Customers' Preferences and Values
Disruptive technologies also destroy existing business models because they reset customers' expectations about value, pricing, and product performance. For example, customers enjoying the benefits of MP3 music files at a price of 99 cents each will never go back to purchasing CDs costing upwards of $12 for a lot of "filler music" that they never really wanted. Digital music files mean that consumers can purchase whatever music they want anytime, anywhere.

Patients undergoing advanced types of heart, lung, intestinal or glandular surgery from physicians using state-of-the-art laser and robotic surgical tools do not have to tolerate the long recovery times of more invasive methods considered cutting-edge just a few years ago. Think of these developments as the "Lasikization" of medicine: eye surgery to correct nearsightedness and cataracts now takes less than an hour to complete. This is the standard that patients now expect when considering surgery for other treatments too. These advanced tools have dramatically speeded up healing time and greatly reduced collateral damage from more traditional surgery techniques. Likewise, the growing convenience of receiving needed drug therapies without frequent doctor visits or painful injections is changing patients' view of medicine. Medicine in particular is at the cusp of offering breakthrough new treatments that combine technologies from various disciplines to deliver truly customized solutions for patients. For example, implanted microchips already have demonstrated great potential to deliver drugs that can replace painful injections. These new devices can deliver crucial drug treatments more reliably and precisely than traditional methods. Potential treatment areas include osteoporosis, diabetes, hormone replacement therapy, and chronic pain management.[3] One can already see how the major pharmaceutical firms, such as Pfizer, Merck, Bristol-Myers Squibb, GlaxoSmithKline and others that have just completed a wave of mergers and acquisitions to consolidate their businesses, are rapidly forced to become Reinventors as newer drugs and delivery systems challenge their existing core competencies.

Smartphones have effectively begun to "disrupt" a host of industries, including stand-alone digital cameras, GPS navigation systems, MP3 music players, and even personal computers. As smartphones become more multifunctional, smaller, sleeker, and elegant in design, they dramatically raise the bar in terms of what customers expect from them. Built-in smartphone cameras now have the resolution and image clarity of point-and-shoot digital cameras. Smartphone hard drives now can store hundreds of MP3 files with convenient features that eliminate the need for stand-alone players. Newer smartphones are so much more capable and versatile that they have the potential to disrupt each industry that they touch and absorb as a feature. For example, as next-generation smartphones incorporate GPS systems, the impact on companies operating in the same field as Garmin and TomTom could be devastating. In all these instances, the "disruption" destroys the rationale for older business models, as Nokia and Research in Motion are now learning to their chagrin.

The Firm's Skills and Knowledge Base
Disruption is as much organizational as it is technological. Reinventors confronting the full impact of disruptive technologies must "unlearn" the organizational practices, processes, routines, and systems that once supported their earlier ways of doing business. Yet, "unlearning" is

clearly one of the most difficult tasks ever to confront an organization. At its core, unlearning is all about tearing down assumptions about how to compete, how to create value, and how to serve the customer. Unlearning mandates that people completely question and relearn their "mental maps" for understanding how their business operates.[4] More often than not, this is a prolonged, painful process that means resetting the priorities for everything that the business does.

Consider the unlearning facing numerous business units at chemical giant DuPont today. The promise of nanotechnology is vast for everything from new types of "engineered plastics," to new types of clothes whose fibers can expand and contract depending on external temperatures, to custom-made engineered materials that may ultimately replace conventional steel and aluminum on aircraft and other vehicles. Nanotechnology represents a completely new field of science that combines molecular-level engineering with biotechnology, advanced engineered materials, and even electronics. Already, numerous scientists and managers at DuPont have had to relearn as they grapple with incorporating nanotechnology techniques into their traditional fibers, polymers, life sciences, and advanced materials businesses. Yet, effective learning of nanotechnology developments and production techniques requires the "unlearning" of older production methods and assumptions about what types of science work best for the future.

Regulatory Changes

There is little doubt that new laws and regulations can radically alter an industry's environment. In the 1970s and 1980s, deregulation of the airline and trucking industries in the United States removed barriers to entry and forced established businesses to completely rethink the way they served their customers as new competitors flooded into the industry. One of the consequential regulatory changes impacting the high-technology and telecommunications industries was the passage of the Telecommunications Act of 1996. This act effectively enabled satellite, cable, telephone, and Internet service providers to enter each other's markets. Deregulation spurred cable companies, such as Time Warner Cable and Cablevision, to offer long-distance and Internet services.

Conversely, AT&T and the local Bell Regional Operating Companies found themselves immediately competing against satellite and cable providers looking to "bundle" all types of communications services into a one-stop shop for consumers. Businesses in each of the impacted industries were catapulted into becoming Reinventors, as they struggled to adapt to a completely new competitive environment.

Unforeseen Competitor

Reinvention is often necessary for survival when established businesses face an entirely new or completely different type of competitor entering the market. General Motors, Ford, and Chrysler found themselves near death's door during the 1970s and 1980s as Toyota, Honda, Nissan, and Mazda entered the U.S. market in a big way. Comfortable with the illusion that American consumers would not purchase imported cars, the Big Three (at the time) languished in complacency as product quality steadily dropped while labor and operating costs rose. Japanese companies, on the other hand, perfected the art of continuous improvement, benchmarking, and total quality management (TQM). These techniques forced all three U.S. automakers to reinvent every aspect of designing and building a car. This reinvention story continues to this very day, as those same companies now must learn how to incorporate ever more advanced hybrid, fuel-cell, and cleaner technologies into their product lines.

The likelihood that more and more people will continue to make most of their purchases online presents significant challenges for established retailers such as Wal-Mart and Target. One can already envision how customers will increasingly rely on online providers to deliver bulky and heavy items, like pet foods, swimming pool chemicals, lawn treatment products, and even home products directly to the front door.

Strategic Issues for Reinventors

As seen from these examples, Reinventors face near life-and-death questions about their viability as ongoing businesses. For Reinventors, the most important answer is to the question: How soon do we inevitably become irrelevant? The issue of reinvention becomes even more salient if one believes that "inflection points" or "disruptions" are becoming more frequent and pronounced in a growing number of industries. Already, we noted that any business in any industry touched by the Internet was forced to reinvent itself to adapt or die. Nowhere has this been more stark than for businesses such as Encyclopedia Britannica (which exists now solely in digital form), Borders (extinct), brokerages (all-feature websites and smartphone apps), retailing (the rise of Amazon), travel agencies (the near extinction of stand-alone travel agencies), banking (smartphone apps), and especially entertainment (the rise of TiVo, Hulu, digital movie rentals, etc.). Imagine the numerous dilemmas and questions now plaguing businesses such as newspapers, book publishers, and network television stations, who are struggling to redefine just exactly what kind of value they represent to customers.

Reinventors, by their very nature, have lost their sources of competitive advantage. Opportunities to distinguish their products or services from their competitors have faded over time as obsolescence sets in. While reinventors may still possess brand names (e.g., Kodak) that conjure up their products' glory days, whatever immediate profits they still generate cannot make up for the consumer drift away from these brands. Their very existence is in question because their pre-existing business models no longer create value. Yet, they are burdened with the legacy of how they previously competed. This "legacy" includes how they produced the product/service, how they organized their activities, and how they managed, evaluated, and rewarded their workforces. Over time, this legacy effect means that businesses facing the need for re-invention are saddled with a pre-existing way of thinking about how to compete and how to create value. The major strategic issues facing Reinventors are shown in Table 7.1.

The cost efficiency-driven strategic disciplines of Consolidators are of no use to Reinventors; in fact, cost efficiency to produce an obsolete or unwanted product can actually accelerate business decline and impede learning. Reinventors cannot attain the degree of technological leadership or customer service intimacy that Trendsetters enjoy. Businesses caught in reinvention mode are unlikely to possess the agility, laser-like

Table 7.1 Key Strategic Issues for Reinventors
• Recognize the impact of disruption on every aspect of the business • Past business success dilutes urgency to change • Previous skill sets and mindsets slow down ability to adapt to new reality

focus, and nimbleness of Pioneers. Since many of today's Reinventors were once Consolidators or Trendsetters prior to an industry "inflection point," they are more than likely burdened with the prevailing "dominant logics" and cognitive biases of competing from earlier time periods.

One needs to go no further than the annals of recent business history to see how numerous firms, many of whom dominated their respective industries, failed to reinvent and to adapt. In the 1970s, we had such well-known consumer electronics firms as Westinghouse Electric, Zenith Electronics, Philco, Thorn-EMI, and Admiral. In retailing, W. T. Grant and A&P faded in the wake of growth of suburban shopping malls and new competitors, as represented by K-Mart and Sears until they themselves eventually became dinosaurs when they were unable to adapt to the new challenges posed by Target and Wal-Mart in later decades. In the 1980s and 1990s, Wang Labs (word processing systems), RCA (a pioneer that created many precursor electronics industries), Beatrice, GAF, and W. R. Grace encountered enormous difficulties and either ceased operations or restructured under the weight of unsustainable financial liabilities.

Death by a Thousand Clicks

Over the past five decades, the story of Xerox embodies the entire spirit and trials of Reinvention. It pioneered "reprographics" (which is a fancy way of saying photocopying) and it became Xerox's core business for the next three decades. From the 1960s to the early 1980s, Xerox enjoyed immense profitability as a wall of patents protected its core technology from rivals. During this same period, Xerox's Palo Alto-based laboratories, known as "Xerox Parc," developed the core technologies that would lay the foundation for the Internet (the Ethernet networking system), for today's easy-to-use personal computers, smartphones, and tablets (the graphical user interface, or else known as computer display icons), and numerous other breakthroughs. Ironically, Xerox never really captured the full value of its cutting-edge technologies and innovations. The company became increasingly reliant on its photocopiers to generate year after year of record profits. Although Xerox possessed enormous technological skill and brainpower, it lacked the vision to commercialize its laboratory breakthroughs into innovative products for new types of customers and markets elsewhere. High profitability insulated senior management from sensing and understanding the looming changes that would inevitably occur after Xerox lost patent protection and new technologies began to make the photocopier less important to customers.

When Xerox lost patent protection in the 1980s, domestic competitors, such as IBM and Eastman Kodak, entered the market with their own powerful photocopiers. More ominously, ultra-efficient competitors from Japan, including Canon, Sharp, Minolta, and Ricoh, entered the U.S. market with smaller, more energy-efficient, and extremely reliable machines that seldom needed repairs. Although Xerox's brand name remained synonymous with high-end innovation for a long time, customers soon replaced their machines with those from Canon and other Japanese rivals. Reeling from merciless Japanese competition, Xerox was forced to reinvent itself by learning and adapting the same manufacturing methods, total quality management systems, and just-in-time supplier relationships from its Japanese rivals. Xerox's turnaround took over eight years before the company stabilized, but it never regained its former glory. Ironically, a good part of Xerox's transformation and reinvention could not have happened without its Japanese joint-venture partner, Fuji-Xerox, which taught Xerox all of the lean manufacturing skills necessary to reinvent its business model and organizational processes. Today, Xerox remains a well-respected name in office products, but it continues to struggle as the whole notion of "photocopying" has given way to e-mail, Postscript-generated documents (e.g., scanning), and digital attachments that completely eliminate all of the vital features provided by traditional photocopiers.

Arenas

No matter the product or service, a dramatic and long-term shift away from the business' current offerings will ultimately occur in many industries. At this point, the focus is on redefining the core business markets in which the firm serves. These markets are often confronted with new competitors offering a more vibrant or more cost-effective substitute, or firms adding a new set of core competencies to create breakthrough value propositions. This means learning a rapidly evolving technology or choosing a new way to add value to customers.

Penguin Books, a major business unit of Pearson PLC, is aware of the need to adapt rapidly to the rise of the market for e-books and e-readers. One of the biggest challenges facing Penguin Books is how to set the prices for digital publications, since much of this content flows through electronic smart devices such as Apple's iPad and other "tablet" appliances. A major question facing Penguin is whether it should adopt "agency pricing," whereby publishers set consumer retail prices but retailers receive a fixed percentage of revenues as payment. Although Penguin relies heavily on existing brick-and-mortar retailers to carry its publishing list of more than 4,000 titles, it is also beginning to invest in new web-based initiatives that will highlight the publishers' newest books, and then sell them directly to consumers. This move has engendered considerable debate within Penguin, as senior managers worry about "cannibalizing" sales in existing distribution channels and relationships with these online initiatives.

Penguin's CEO John Makinson believes that there will be two different arenas in which it must compete: the book reader and the book owner. The book reader enjoys reading and will purchase a digital version without hesitation. Penguin believes that the book reader will probably gravitate towards the very inexpensive, self-published titles that now populate Amazon's Kindle and Barnes & Noble's Nook e-readers. However, the book reader will not represent the traditional type of customer that keeps, shares, and displays physical books in his or her home or office—the book owner, in other words. The book owner remains very attractive to Penguin, and the publisher is seeking to enhance its books by making them more physically attractive. This step also enables Penguin to raise the price for this latter type of customer.

Over the long term, Makinson concedes that there will be a dramatic reduction in the number of brick-and-mortar bookstores and that Penguin must prepare itself for the day when book owners who still shop at independent bookstores will be a very small portion of the total market.[5] To ensure that it can continue to learn new technologies, Penguin and other Pearson-owned book units will merge with Random House, a unit of Bertelsmann, to better compete with other publishers.[6]

In the arena of high-technology office products, Xerox continues to reinvent itself. It is in the midst of a major transformation as it seeks to further de-emphasize its reliance on photocopiers, a business where, as noted above, margins are rapidly disappearing as e-documents displace the need for physical documents in the workplace. CEO Ursula Burns is in the fourth year of major efforts to redefine Xerox as a services-based business whereby Xerox runs the back-office operations of other large businesses, while providing important technologies and products to help make better documents. In 2012, the services business brought in more than half of Xerox's total revenues. Still, Burns acknowledges that Xerox will continue to remain a player in color printing, especially in the arena of what Xerox terms its "Document Outsourcing Business." This Xerox business unit, which seeks to combine the production of color copiers and business services, focuses on managing the internal printing needs of large organizations and corporate customers. The biggest driver of Xerox's future services business, according to Burns, will be business process outsourcing. In this business, Xerox will handle much of the internal "paperwork" and processes related to customers' payroll, inventory tracking, supply chain management, compliance, and other cost-center activities.[7] The arena-related issues confronting Reinventors are found in Table 7.2.

Table 7.2 Key Arena Issues for Reinventors

- Served market undergoes massive upheaval
- Newly emerging rivals are faster, more aggressive
- Identifying new value propositions hard to execute

Vehicles

If C-level executives know that they need to enter a new business, how are they going to accomplish that? Are they going to rely on internal product development, or are there other vehicles that they can pursue to achieve their changed product scope? There is a steep learning curve associated with each vehicle, so what are some costs of learning?

Strategic alliances represent complementary external vehicles for Reinventors. Partners that possess important cutting-edge technologies or practice advanced management techniques can become vital repositories of knowledge for Reinventors to learn from. These alliances enable the firm to reduce many internal costs and risks of going it alone. Alliances also help it gain vital insight of a technology's or market's future direction from an experienced partner, just as Fuji-Xerox enabled Xerox to learn new skills in lean manufacturing.

Procter & Gamble, despite its enormous market success, is not taking any chances about its future. P&G realizes that marketing to consumers in the future will be very different, as network television, print media, and traditional distribution channels begin to lose their appeal to customers. The company spends billions annually to promote its products, but is worried that fewer customers are hearing P&G's messages as they tune out advertising on television and road-side billboards. As a result, P&G is now beefing up its digital media operations to learn everything about search-engine marketing, online advertising, Twitter, and YouTube. P&G has formed important alliances with Google, Microsoft, Yahoo, and Facebook in order to exchange ideas, insights, and ad-based technologies. It also seeks to keep abreast and learn about all aspects of digital marketing through both its internal digital media operations, as well as through its alliance partners. Ironically, some of P&G's most innovative digital initiatives have come from those products that traditionally received very little money, such as Aussie Hair Care and Secret deodorant, both of whom are marketed and promoted entirely through digital channels.[8] The vehicles that Reinventors can use to support their strategy are depicted in Table 7.3.

Table 7.3 Key Vehicle Issues for Reinventors
• Alliances enable business to learn new skills, knowledge • Internal development often hamstrung by obsolete assumptions and mindsets • Big acquisitions risk taking the business along unknown routes

Staging

Reinventors must develop new products and enter new markets as they learn and assimilate new technologies. This learning process is often difficult and takes time. Thus, staging for Reinventors will entail firms' experimenting with new products as they are learning what their customers truly want. Because Reinventors are confronting unfamiliar new technologies, they cannot afford to bet the entire business on the choice of a single technology or product to transform themselves; such a move is fraught with danger. The business may find itself choosing an unproven, risky technology, or worse still, selecting a technical standard that the rest of the industry has abandoned.

National Geographic faces a number of strategic conundrums as it realizes the need to confront and embrace a digital future. Best known for its eponymous magazine that features bold, breathtaking photographs of some of the world's most isolated and beautiful locations, the company's English-language circulation has fallen by more than half since the 1980s. The 125-year-old firm is now seeking to expand the magazine's reach through multiple technological platforms, including websites, new types of television offerings, and even testing the video-game market. CEO John Fahey also knows that he must keep *National Geographic* relevant to increasing numbers of readers who rely primarily on their iPad, Kindle, and other e-readers and tablets.

To reach larger numbers of digital-only customers, Fahey is experimenting with the use of blogs to keep the magazine up to date on a daily and even hourly basis. The company believes that *National Geographic* must reinvent itself from a once-a-month subscription to the equivalent of a digital "app" whereby readers can access the magazine's enormous library of maps, stories, photographs, and video on a real-time basis. CEO Fahey hopes that the magazine's content will be updated constantly as readers communicate with the publisher, other readers, and external blogs about day-to-day events and changes about the earth's environment and other developments. To keep *National Geographic* up to date, the company has hired hundreds of contract employees whose job is to photograph and make new films about places around the world. Some of these bloggers will even engage in video production work, which—if suitable in quality—will be featured in the print magazine and on the website itself too. Thus, National Geographic's approach to hiring external bloggers represents an important staging move that allows the magazine to test what kind of content will be best suited for its publications without the risk of hiring too many full-time employees.

National Geographic also hopes to reach a younger audience in the future, as most existing subscribers are currently in their fifties. To extend the magazine's appeal and reach, the firm is considering creating video games, and is offering a newly bundled subscription that includes print, access to all photographic archives, and the digital edition as well. Ultimately, CEO Fahey believes that the print edition will no longer exist, even if not until in the far future, and that the company must prepare for that ultimate reality.[9]

The printing presses have completed shut down for *Newsweek*, once a leading weekly magazine that offered news on politics, international affairs, sports, and business. After having been in business for over a century, *Newsweek*'s subscribers migrated to other online sources of news and commentary—the Huffington Post and Real Clear Politics, for example—as well as other websites that could provide more timely and instantaneous updates of their interests. Table 7.4 outlines the staging of strategic activities for Reinventors.

Distinction

Because disruption renders the Reinventors' prior technologies, processes, and customer bases obsolete, Reinventors must often start from scratch. They have little distinction and often are behind other

Table 7.4 Key Staging Issues for Reinventors
• Experiment with new product designs • Commit to unproven technologies slowly • Explore new niches as platform to learn customer needs

Pioneers and Trendsetters that have redefined the marketplace in their favor. How will they win in the marketplace? For all businesses, success is the result of creating distinction and C-level executives must make tradeoffs about where to deploy resources to achieve that. Will it be through proprietary products and processes, unparalleled service, highest quality, brand image, or lowest price?

Consider the case of Fujifilm, which faced many of same challenges of technological obsolescence that confronted its most important rival, Eastman Kodak. Unlike Kodak, Fujifilm realized that its core film product would eventually become irrelevant. Fujifilm possessed a deep reservoir of competencies and knowledge in chemistry and "surface-action science," which describes how to chemically treat a surface with new types of materials. Using the skills and insights it learned from making better-resolution films over four decades, Fujifilm applied the same insight to develop advanced "surface-action" materials that found their way into drugs, LCD panels, and even cosmetics. Through its long experience with film chemistry, Fujifilm realized that the chemical treatment proprietary processes that were used to prevent film images from fading can also be used to enhance the skin.

Fujifilm's reinvention efforts were a hard sell within the firm, however. Film manufacturing facilities were shut down and thousands of employees lost their jobs. CEO Shigetaka Komori knew that his firm was in a race for its life. In 2000 Komori immediately shifted the still-high profitability of camera film to new business ventures that could readily benefit from Fujifilm's chemistry-based core competencies. Fujifilm spent heavily to learn about crafting ultra-thin layers of film using new chemical compounds from its labs. As a result, one of

Fujifilm's most important businesses now is the use of an ultra-thin film to serve as the electronic backdrop of LCD panels for computers, televisions, and other appliance screens.

On a related front, Fujifilm has also become an important supplier of chemicals and thin-film technologies that are used in the pharmaceutical industry. Its R&D team is examining ways to make drugs more readily absorbed by the human body, while other research initiatives have developed skin-care products using anti-oxidation technologies. In 2012, Fujifilm derived less than 1 per cent of its revenue from photographic film, down from nearly 20 per cent a decade ago and almost 30 per cent in the early 1990s. CEO Komori credits Fujifilm's turnaround to its urgent transformation efforts that leveraged what it always did well: a new arena that focused on chemical compounds that opened the way to much broader applications than just film, and capitalized on Fuji's sources of distinction.[10]

Milliken, a leading U.S. manufacturer of textiles and fibers, faced enormous problems competing in an industry that has long suffered under the weight of cheap textile imports from Asia and rising U.S. labor costs. Milliken realized it needed to create new sources of distinction in its core textile fiber business to compete. Two decades ago, the textile landscape in states such as North and South Carolina, Virginia, and Georgia, was dominated by large, labor-intensive mills that churned out yarn, cotton, and other fibers for the clothing and apparel industry. No U.S. firm, including Milliken, could offer its customers anything distinctive, nor were any of their manufacturing operations cost-efficient, superior in quality, or in any way better than their foreign rivals. Yet, Milliken has thrived by refining and improving its fiber technology to the point where it became an active supplier of advanced fibers to other industries (e.g., military applications, energy, adhesives). Instead of completely abandoning the textile and fiber business, Milliken spent much of the 1990s redefining its identity and core business around creating and designing new kinds of engineered and reinforced fibers. It has now achieved distinction in all types of fiber-related technologies and has the upper hand when coming up with new product ideas. These have ultimately found their use in such diverse products as reinforced duct tape, magic markers, fire-retardant mattresses, and even combat gear. Even more advanced fibers are now used to coat windmill blades and provide anti-microbial protection to kitchen countertops. Milliken's senior management galvanized the company's research efforts to the point where it now commands thousands of patents on specialty fibers that can be used in almost any possible application. The company likes to boast that the average person comes in contact with a Milliken innovation some 50 times a day. Milliken's stunning reinvention has even led it to open up a new manufacturing innovation center that aims to teach other companies how to revitalize and transform their operations in the wake of major technological change or intense price competition from abroad.[11] The critical sources of distinction underpinning a Reinventor's strategy are shown in Table 7.5.

Economic Logic

Reinventors are faced with the ultimate question when it comes to economic logic: Can the business ultimately earn a return on capital that exceeds its cost? In many instances, the answer is "no", and the change effort fails. All Reinventors need to ask themselves whether they can ultimately create something distinctive (product, technology, new process) and earn a return that justifies this investment.

Consider the situation now facing Pfizer, one of the world's best known drug companies and a creator of leading brands across the drug categories it dominates. Pfizer and other pharmaceutical firms realize that the days in which they enjoy long patent protection for breakthrough drugs are over. Drug firms face the prospect of surviving a "perfect storm" of three simultaneous challenges. First, they are now

---

Table 7.5 Ways to Achieve Distinction for Reinventors

- Start from a "clean sheet" approach
- Confront the reality of the new competitive environment
- Divert existing cash flow into new business prospects

witnessing new disruptive technologies and innovations encroaching on their businesses. New genomic sequencing techniques, nanotechnology advances, and genetic-based therapies have begun to displace traditional antibiotics and other mainstay treatment regimens. Many of these innovations have sprung forth not only from Pioneering biotechnology and nanotechnology firms, but also from computer and software companies that possess the encryption-type skills needed to unlock genetic codes and sequences. Second, new competitors springing up internationally are giving U. S. companies a run for their money as they, too, learn and amass the vital R&D skills that make them formidable competitors. Teva Pharmaceutical in Israel, as well as Ranbaxy and Dr. Reddy Labs in India, represent the new face of low-cost competitors. Their lower cost structures also enable them to compete more ferociously for market share, especially in emerging markets where strong price controls over drugs dictate choice of treatment. Third, the increasing scope and intensity of government regulation in the U.S. complicate the pharmaceutical industry's visibility for future product development. The specter of possible price controls, as well as strict federal oversight that may unfold from the Affordable Care Act (known colloquially as "ObamaCare"), makes it hard for drug firms to assess what products they should concentrate their efforts on, as well as to chart the path for future investments that will facilitate the innovation of powerhouse new drugs.[12]

Consequently, Pfizer has decided that its future will no longer be dedicated to creating breakthrough drugs that serve the mass market. Instead, it will focus its research on niche-market drugs that treat thousands of patients. Pfizer is moving away from developing such enormous blockbusters as cholesterol statin Lipitor and blood pressure drug Norvasc. In the past, Pfizer spent billions on designing, testing, and commercializing these drugs. In today's environment, it is ever more difficult for drug companies to obtain the regulatory approval and reimbursement needed for a wide array of drugs. Previously, Pfizer would have never pursued a drug whose potential use limited it to a small number of patients; it simply would have never been able to recoup its investment. Now, however, the company has completely revamped its business model and is focusing on those new drugs where there are fewer competitors. By focusing on harder-to-treat ailments, it is believed that this economic logic to drug development will help Pfizer capture billions in sales of new drugs.[13]

As might be expected, other drug companies are taking a different tack to meeting the challenges of the future. Merck committed over $8 billion in R&D in 2011 and looks to increase that amount as it pursues new drug development through a variety of vehicles: internal development as well as co-development with smaller, biotechnology-oriented firms. Even though drug development is an inherently risky process, Merck believes that only further research and commitment can help the company grow in the long term.[14]

Intel faces the prospect of significant disruption in its core business of building the microprocessors for today's personal computers. The crucial question facing Intel about the future? What will the company do now that customers are shying away from PCs and beginning to use electronic tablets, smartphones, and other yet-to-be-seen digital appliances? Intel continues to remain profitable and is the envy of its semiconductor rivals. Yet, Intel remains famous for questioning everything it does, taking a page from former CEO Grove's "you can't be too paranoid" stance. Realizing that it must change the economic logic of its business before it is too late, Intel does not want to be caught in the quagmire of declining personal computer sales. Instead, Intel is revamping its product development and business model to de-emphasize high-speed chip performance for its own sake. Using its exceptional proprietary manufacturing processes, Intel announced a major shift in chip development strategy as it focuses its efforts on making ever more efficient power-consuming chips. Intel is banking on a completely different vision of how people merge computing with smaller communication devices. This is a new business that Intel must navigate carefully. By slicing each chip's power consumption, Intel hopes that it can muscle its way into becoming a leading supplier to tablet and smartphone manufacturers. Current Intel chips remain unsuitable for buyers in these industries, since Intel's existing line generates too much heat and drains battery life. CEO Paul Otellini considers Intel's current moves to be as significant and company-changing as the efforts made by Andy Grove to create the breakthrough line of Pentium processors for PCs and Centrino chips for laptops in the mid-1990s.[15] Intel believes it has an excellent vantage point to create these power-efficient chips as it possesses a unique and deep set of manufacturing skills that enable it to quickly adjust its factories according to the chip's specifications. This gives the firm a leg-up on other chip companies that outsource to "chip foundries" to make up for their lack of in-house production.[16] Yet, Intel must remain vigilant about such smaller competitors as ARM Holdings and Qualcomm. Intel's chips have an inherent advantage in running Microsoft's Windows-based systems, but Microsoft has little competitive advantage in the emerging tablet market, whose underlying software is dominated by Apple and Google's Android operating system. Intel is counting on its manufacturing muscle to help it gain even more market share once the smartphone and electronic tablet markets become more mature.[17]

Strategic Discipline: Proactive Resource Allocation

Successful reinvention means that businesses must acknowledge the shifting industry landscape's impact on their competitive advantage. Undertaking reinvention is not without its risks—in fact, the entire reinvention process is all about managing risks on multiple dimensions: sorting through customers' changing needs; understanding new technologies; learning and cultivating new organizational processes; and instilling new skills, cultures, and mindsets throughout the firm. Failure to deliver on any of those fronts spells an end to reinvention. To cope and embrace the new reality, Reinventors need to clearly set priorities for their transformation along three critical paths:

1. define the core business;
2. exploring the future with small bets;
3. manage the transfer pricing process.

Define the Core Business

Central to successful reinvention is a total, organization-wide commitment to define and invest in the future core business. As seen from the

Fujifilm, Milliken, and Intel examples, Reinventors need to ask themselves hard questions about what are their core competencies, and how these core competencies can create future growth opportunities. All too often, managers define a core business as one that has been profitable for a long time. This is overly superficial thinking. A business became profitable at some point during the firm's existence because it delivered compelling value to the customer and distinguished itself from rivals in important ways. Unfortunately, the business' steady stream of profits and cash engenders a "cruise-control" mentality in managers. They expect that the business will continue to deliver annual profit gains without realizing that the ingredients of a successful business often need ongoing careful refinement; without it, they can wither from neglect.

According to Gary Hamel and C. K. Prahalad, two management theorists, the "roots" of any business are the deep skills, technologies, and organizational processes that work in tandem to promote innovation.[18] From this perspective, the definition of a core business is not tied to a specific product's identity, but more about how the business goes about systematically creating opportunities for the future.

One company that has continuously reinvented itself over the century of its existence is U.S. industrial giant 3M. Starting out as a sandpaper manufacturer, 3M realized that it could invent new products based on how well it was able to layer paper, film, or other surfaces with varying degrees of adhesive chemical compounds and treatments. While perhaps best known today for its Post-it Notes, Scotch Tape, and Scotchgard fabric treatments, 3M is constantly innovating. Hiring some of the most inquisitive and creative personnel from all types of scientific backgrounds, 3M has accumulated tens of thousands of patents on anything related to adhesives, membranes, filters, thin films, and even composite materials. It is now a leading provider of ingredients and products to the automotive, aerospace, health care, office products, and even pharmaceutical industries. 3M touches the day-to-day lives of many consumers without them even realizing, since many of its patents cover everything from how compact discs play music to the filters they use to trap dust in their air-conditioning systems.

How does 3M thrive when so many of its products face rapid maturity and low-price competition? The company believes that resources should be allocated to wherever the best ideas emanate from anywhere in the organization. To promote innovation and the fast growth of profitable businesses, 3M is convinced that its technologies and ideas belong to everyone in the organization. Profits earned from new products belong to those who take the risk to make them into stand-alone businesses. In other words, anyone, anywhere, at 3M is free to experiment with any type of technology. Their business unit can freely profit from it if they are willing to take the risk of making it work. People at 3M are even free to spend up to 20 per cent of their time working on their favored project ideas.[19] A new technology that "fails" in one business can become a "success" in another. Personnel experimenting with the "failed" idea are not sanctioned, and in fact, encouraged to utilize their zeal and insight to keep identifying and searching for new prospects. This approach to encouraging new idea formation was the basis for Post-it Notes' ultimate success as a big 3M business.

Novo Nordisk stayed true to its roots in insulin innovation even as the Danish company faced rising competition from the large pharmaceutical firms that introduced a wide array of new types of diabetes pills over the past decade. Although the overall market for diabetes-related treatments is growing, Novo was losing ground as better-funded drug makers crafted new types of pill-based regimens that eroded Novo's market share in selling injectable insulin. CEO Lars Rebien Sørenson took the dramatic steps of ceasing all of Novo's research into pill-based treatments and redoubling the company's efforts to improve the molecular structure of insulin itself. Novo's "designer insulin" products involve adjusting the protein's chemical structure so that it works faster and longer. Over the past decade, Novo's profitability has surged and its diabetes treatment has become the gold standard that other rivals have tried to emulate.[20] This was done by refining its core business.

Exploring the Future with Small Bets

Reinventors face the delicate balancing act of harvesting the profitability of its existing businesses while investing in promising business opportunities. Cash from a mature business serves as the fuel for experi-mentation, learning, and exploration. Reinventors must explore their possible futures by carefully investing in small bets that limit their downside risk in case they misjudge the future marketplace, technology, or customer needs.

A promising vehicle that helps Reinventors explore a new market is to rely on small units (skunkworks) that serve as "incubators" of prom-ising ideas and technologies. Firms throughout the entertainment, high-technology, resource-exploration, life-science, and energy busi-nesses have long used a variety of small units to "prospect" for future growth.[21] In some instances, firms in these industries will buy a small equity stake in promising start-up ventures (often Pioneers in an emerging technology), hoping to take advantage of the future upside while locking in their downside risk. The underlying theory behind the use of "strategic real options" is that organizations can place bets whose value rises and falls depending on whether the uncertainty confronting them is favorable or unfavorable. Large firms often form internal "venture capital" financing arms whose sole purpose is to identify Pioneers that possess new technologies and growth ideas early on. If a Pioneer succeeds with its product idea, the larger firm will then increase its bet on it, or even acquire it outright. This is the strategy long pursued by Cisco Systems as it seeks to learn new technologies and acquire smaller companies that possess the seeds of future business ideas.

Over the past few years, General Motors has invested close to $100 million in start-up companies developing potentially break-through technologies. GM believes that providing seed money is a vital ingredient in its attempts to resuscitate its automotive operations and to learn the vital technologies underpinning advanced engines, electronics, and alternative energy concepts. Under GM's investment deals, the company is able to take advantage of the technological gains and profits if the start-up succeeds. The EN-V concept, an electric car that spots and then avoids collisions—and which can also drive and park itself—is a Chevrolet "skunkworks" project. In addition, GM receives preferred first access to the new technology before the company can sell it to other firms, including GM's rivals. Areas of intense GM focus include batteries, fuel-free engines, and even digital electronics that form the basis for next-generation dashboards and automotive entertainment systems.[22]

Realizing that its sales have plateaued and that generic drug competition is taking a bigger bite of its profits, Andrew Witty, CEO of the drug giant GlaxoSmithKline (GSK), acknowledged that the company became complacent during the past decade when it earned record profitability from such breakthrough drugs as Advair, Avandia, and Wellbutrin. After participating in the massive industry consolidation, GSK is seeking to reinvent itself before it loses even more ground. Now, CEO Witty has completely upended GSK's entire approach to drug development. Instead of spending nearly $6 billion annually on R&D, GSK has created over 40 small biotech-oriented units that have considerable autonomy to chart their own research without bureaucratic oversight. These units are charged with focusing their efforts on the high-risk, high-return sciences that were the domain of Pioneering biotechnology firms a few years ago.

GSK is also becoming more proactive in acquiring smaller drug companies that have partnered with the company on previous drug projects. In 2012, GSK announced its purchase of Human Genome Sciences, a company with which it had been developing a new treatment for lupus. GSK has also targeted Pioneers with promising basic science research, even when their commercial prospects were uncertain. For example, in 2008, it acquired Sirtis for $720 million. Sirtis works on drugs to slow down age-related diseases. To broaden its exploratory scope, GSK also actively licenses new drug technology from small Pioneers such as Anacor Pharmaceuticals (which is using new chemical bonds to treat antibiotic-resistant bacteria).[23]

Managing the Transfer Pricing Process

As Reinventors shift funds from their mature business to promising new opportunities, they must rethink their ideas on profitability and return on investment (ROI). Transferring resources from one business to another has always tended to be a complicated task in any organization, but it is especially problematic for Reinventors. The major issue is to allocate cash from existing mature business(es) to uncertain new ventures that consume cash quickly. We know that senior managers are likely to be extremely risk-averse when it comes to allocating funds to a new business, product idea, or technology they do not understand. We also know these same managers are probably unaware of what benchmarks (e.g., ROE, ROI, market share gains) should be used when measuring the financial progress of their new ventures. Cost-efficiency metrics that drive and reinforce low-cost operations, for example, do not apply, nor do they fit the need to prospect and experiment. Thus, Reinventors must clearly specify and execute the transfer pricing mechanism and accountability measures across various units.

Transfer prices are tricky for several reasons. In some instances, firms will try to maintain an artificially low cost of capital for their "core" businesses, while starving their new ventures businesses of badly needed funds. It is easy for senior management to argue and justify such reasoning, since the core business probably enjoys the longest history within the firm, has a more established record of profitability, and has been the business unit where future leaders were groomed and developed. Core businesses that enjoy a long history of creating earlier technologies, desirable products, and well-regarded brands command a "moral high ground" in many organizations. It is difficult to argue with previous success, especially when the full effect of an "inflection point" has yet to be felt. Ironically, this tilts the firm toward investing in arenas that begin to lose their distinction. Senior managers may continue their bias of allocating ever greater resources to core businesses. This can lead to the paradoxical effect that insulates the core business from the urgency of unlearning existing practices and cultivating new ones. "Core" businesses continue to look profitable from a financial perspective, while in practice their real rate of return is indeed lower.

Distorted transfer pricing can sometimes work in the other direction as well. In other instances, senior management can tilt the transfer pricing equation the other way by overly subsidizing new ventures for too long. Because significant uncertainty overshadows the futures of new ventures, an overly generous bias in their favor may result in "throwing good money after bad." Managers often escalate their commitment to a new technology that may prove unworkable. This has the deleterious effect of pouring money into prospects that are unlikely to ever meet the firm's economic logic criteria. In the 1980s, General Motors faced this problem when it created dozens of new ventures and alliances to learn about ways to make dashboards smarter and its factories more flexible. GM also spent billions to find ways to upgrade automotive windshields to become more like aircraft heads-up displays (HUDs), built entirely new automated factories with cutting-edge artificial intelligence, and even tested the use of ceramic materials to replace metal-based engines. Most of these ventures produced interesting scientific breakthroughs but they never proved cost effective for full-scale commercialization.

We may be witnessing a similar replay of this economic situation now. Global automotive businesses are spending prodigious amounts of resources experimenting with new forms of "smart" technology that have the promise to transform how cars interact with the driver, other cars, and even large-scale urban traffic management systems through "cloud computing" techniques. Automakers are seeking ways to incorporate more web-based technologies into next-generation cars, but most of them do not possess the strong technical skills they need to do this on their own. As they create new units and alliances to learn more about this emerging technology, they run the risk of misjudging what types of software, electronics, and other technical features may best suit the specific needs of the driver. Although these efforts are likely to produce interesting new research, it remains to be seen whether all of these efforts will yield cost-effective products and technologies that customers will be willing to pay for.

Avoid Falling into the Dinosaur Pit

Reinventors are at great risk of "falling into the dinosaur pit." As they become relics of a previous competitive time period, Reinventors must act quickly to embrace a new future while unlearning their pre-existing organizational practices and mindsets. We have identified the three primary organizational issues confronting Reinventors:

1. denial;
2. existing hierarchy vs. new unit;
3. reward systems.

The strategic vulnerabilities facing Reinventors are summarized in Table 7.6.

Denial

Large firms attempting reinvention often fall into the dinosaur trap because they wait too long to aggressively address their internal challenges. Denial occurs everywhere in human life, especially in large organizations where it is all too easy for senior management to bury their heads in the proverbial sand. Executives can find any number of ways to rationalize a core business' declining performance: "unfair" competition; the new technology is a "fad"; our customers won't go for the new idea; if the idea is so promising, why didn't we invent it to begin with; how can anyone argue with our record profitability; our problem is that our costs are too high, etc. One can write endlessly about the ways that smart people can justify their adherence to the past—a justification that becomes ever more rigid with what was tied to the past. Executives may also choose to delay reinvention efforts for fear that new products will cannibalize their existing mature businesses. This fear prevented Eastman Kodak from taking the drastic steps necessary to learn digital technologies before the camera film business completely collapsed. Having declared bankruptcy in late 2011, Kodak is currently selling what is left of its camera film and document imaging businesses to meet creditor demands in bankruptcy court. Now, all that is left of

---

Table 7.6 Perils of Reinventors

- The longer the denial, the more likely the demise
- House new business endeavors in separate small units
- Force changes in reward systems to instill change

Eastman Kodak's dinosaur bones is its patent portfolio—a sad end to a company that invented the digital camera in 1976 but never could commercialize it.

Denial comes in many forms, but it ultimately costs Reinventors precious time. Successful Reinventors know they must make brutally tough decisions and even the pull the plug on what was once a core business, as Novo Nordisk did with its diabetes pills and Intel did with its memory chips. Of course, these decisions at the time are enormously unpopular, since they inevitably trigger layoffs and much soul-searching. But a spike in short-term pain is far better than thrashing around in the morass of a pit that eventually becomes a lost burial site.

Consider the travails currently facing large Japanese companies. As they continue to lose their grip and influence on all realms of digital consumer electronics, firms such as Sharp, Panasonic, Hitachi, Sony, and Toshiba, have continued to delay badly needed transformation efforts over much of the past decade. In 2012, Japan's top three television producers—Sony, Sharp, and Panasonic—projected losses totaling over $20 billion. Only in 2011 did Hitachi decide, for example, to outsource production of all television sets—a business where it offered nothing truly distinctive.

Sony Corporation's latest CEO, Kazuo Hirai, has promised to revive the company after a decade-long period in which the company squandered its lead in television sets, LCD panels, Playstation video-game consoles, and other once innovative products. CEO Hirai hopes to instill a deep sense of urgency throughout Sony to turn around its unprofitable business. Yet, Sony remains a proud company, with many long-serving executives who still cling to previous ideas and methods about how best to develop new products. The glory days of the Mini-Discman, Walkman, and Trinitron television sets still shape their thinking. In the past, Sony would develop cutting-edge products in its labs and encourage divisions to compete with one another to find the best ones. But Sony fervently believed it could do all of this without much consumer input. This worked during the 1970s and 1980s when Sony's brand name symbolized quality and innovation; consumers thought the company knew best. With the advent of the Internet, however, consumers began to change the way they looked at purchasing music, appliances, and how they used them. Ironically, its core legacy television business, in particular, has proved devastating to Sony, as it was late to adapt to LCD panels. By the time it did so, the company lost its lead to more agile rivals, such as Samsung and LG of South Korea. Sony even depended on rival Samsung to produce the latest generation of LCD panels that it could not create itself. Perhaps most important, Sony completely missed the revolution in how consumers access, purchase, listen, and share music through new Internet-driven devices. Sony lost both its technology and brand leadership as senior management debated incessantly about what route to pursue. This created a huge opening for Apple's series of iPod and iPad appliances, as well as Google's Android operating system that now powers many competing devices from Samsung, HTC, Motorola and others. CEO Hirai recently announced that Sony would concentrate its efforts on its future core businesses—mobile devices, digital cameras, and video-game consoles. Stunningly absent from his announcement was the decision that televisions would remain a core business.[24]

Existing Hierarchy vs. New Unit

Reinventors also face another dilemma. Should they attempt to foster and commercialize a potentially disruptive innovation within their existing organizational structure (hierarchy), or should they design a completely separate new unit? While considerable debate exists, we suggest that established firms are better off incubating promising breakthrough ideas in a new unit at some remove from existing large units. High autonomy accords the new unit much greater leeway in making faster decisions, developing its own identity, and hiring people with fresh ideas without having to justify each decision in existing bureaucracies. New units also benefit from possessing more "organic" organization designs, in which information flows more efficiently, management layers stay much flatter, and execution occurs more promptly. In contrast, older businesses tend to become rigid over time, not only in their organizational structure, but especially in the way C-level executives think and act.

Creating a highly autonomous new unit generates many potential benefits. First, the new unit is free to experiment and prospect new technologies and product ideas at its own rate. Building future competitiveness means that the unit must focus its attention on learning new knowledge and skills from external sources, rather than constantly fighting internal battles with managers from the existing mature business who may not understand the emerging technology.

Second, if the personnel in the new venture are compelled to report through established organizational channels, there exists significant risk that senior managers, who do not understand the venture's technologies or ideas, may impede the unit's progress and ability to learn. Managers from the new venture will possess mindsets, mental maps, and biases that differ greatly from that of their counterparts in the mature business. These senior managers may fear for their own jobs when the firm ultimately adapts to the new competitive reality and begins to allocate fewer resources to the mature business. In turn, they can delay and even potentially sabotage the new unit's learning efforts.

Third, the economic logic used to measure performance in the new venture is likely to be very different from those used in existing mature businesses. Mature businesses are usually highly profitable and generate large amounts of cash flow. Their plant and equipment are largely paid for, their brand names are well-established, and they enjoy stable relationships with distributors and vendors that make financial planning a routine exercise. Consequently, senior managers typically use economic logic based on how well these businesses continue to generate cash, which in turn is usually used to increase dividends to shareholders. On the other hand, new businesses consume cash. They may ultimately reach high profitability, but they must spend cash to build new facilities, hire and develop a workforce, and invest heavily in products and brands that they hope will capture and keep customer loyalty. Blindly using the same economic logic for mature *and* new businesses destroys the incentives in both.

As mentioned earlier, GSK is banking its future on its attempt to become a much smaller, more nimble company through its creation of 40 smaller business units, with each enjoying significant autonomy.

General Motors also keeps its distance from the start-up businesses in which it invests to ensure that the start-up has the discretion to pursue new technology roadmaps unhindered. Realizing that disruption will become a natural part of doing business, General Electric resuscitated its own venture capital arm as well. GE is allocating money to promising businesses in the renewable energy and health-care businesses but keeping its distance from day-to-day management of these businesses. GE realizes that it cannot cover all the bases of advanced technologies through its own large business units. The skills, insights, and approaches GE seeks to develop in the managers running its large mature businesses (e.g., operational excellence, financial acumen) are very different from those needed in new ventures that experiment and think "out-of-the-box" (e.g., R&D, creativity). Even Silicon Valley giant Google is getting into the act. Google acknowledges that it has grown so fast that it cannot possibly stay abreast of every new and potentially disruptive technology that may arrive from unexpected places and arenas. Over the past few years, Google has tried to keep the organization from becoming too bureaucratic in order to preserve the high level of individual creativity that has been the basis for much of the firm's growth and appeal to new talent.

Reward Systems

Strategy execution is a direct function of incentives. Without the proper reward systems in place, organizational chaos, waste, and indecision prevail. All too often, organizations design brilliant strategies, only to see them fail miserably when managers and employees do not understand them, and more importantly, do not commit to them. The seeds for either successfully adapting to a disruption, or creating a disruptive innovation, rest entirely on encouraging breakthrough thinking, decisive action, and risk-taking at all levels.

Several years ago, Brooklyn Union Gas Company (rebranded as KeySpan Energy) decided to enter the consumer market for gas appliances (e.g., stoves and refrigerators) in Brooklyn, New York. The company had previously been focused on the supply of gas to local homes and commercial establishments. In order to attract talented people to leave the parent company so that this new business venture could be formed, BUG needed to redesign its compensation system, which was based on the Hay Point System. BUG rented space from a building across the street from its headquarters and staffed the new operation with employees from the parent firm. It became immediately apparent that a new reward system would be needed because the previous system of counting turn-ons, turn-offs, heating and cooling complaints would not reward the new behaviors—sales of appliances— it needed. Therefore, the managers in the new system were rewarded like employees at The Home Depot, Lowe's and other stores that sold appliances: that is, by units sold. Unfortunately, BUG did not understand the marketplace, the supply chain, and the logistical problems of selling and repairing appliances. The pricing responses from established retailers forced BUG to disband its effort within 24 months.

Reinvention can happen only when there exists a reward system that encourages, rewards, and reinforces the desired behaviors that accompany unlearning. Reward systems function only to the extent that they have an immediate effect, are certain in their application, and consistent in their treatment. Companies failing to reinvent themselves are often unable to design reward systems that meet all three tests.

Bold transformation efforts typically require sustained investment. We recommend that funding should come from the executive suite because only those people can rise above the fray of typical divisional allocations. C-level executives must also avoid the "innovation tax" approach where the C-suite asks all divisions to contribute a percentage of their budgets to such initiatives. Divisional managers seldom see their contribution going toward the good of the company. They simply perceive C-level executives as siphoning off a percentage of their budget in order to save a dying division.[25]

Reinvention requires that C-level executives clearly communicate and remain relentless in the pursuit of strategic goals. There is no getting around the fact that reward systems must change. What is essential is that executives need to identify and accelerate the funding of the most promising initiatives and reduce their commitment to those that, while they remain viable, do not represent the best fit or use of resources and/or core competencies. Changing the reward system sends a clear message.

In our assessment, we believe that successful reinvention can occur only when senior managers are willing to confront problems and potential dangers before they occur. *The more willingly that management runs toward the problem earlier, the less threatening the problem will ultimately become.* The first step to successful unlearning is recognizing that other firms can be far superior to what you do. No one has a monopoly on superior products, technologies, and ways of doing things. The imperative for unlearning is directly related to how entrenched the "Not-Invented-Here (NIH) Syndrome" pervades the business. Businesses led by senior managers who genuinely believe that they have all the answers about what customers want and how to compete are the most vulnerable to disruption. It is akin to the Icarus Paradox, where the arrogant youth's wax wings melted when he flew too close to the sun.

MASTERING THE ESSENTIALS OF A REINVENTOR

Mastering the essentials of a reinventor involves:

- recognizing that disruptive change means the firm must unlearn everything that it has done heretofore;
- disruptive change means you start at square one;
- mature businesses' profitability may seduce managers into ignoring important changes in customer need or in new technology;
- understanding that successful reinvention depends on redesigning the firm's reward systems to promote necessary "unlearning" and organizational change;
- recognizing that failure to change means extinction;

and avoiding the following:

- believing that currently high cash flows are synonymous with a strong competitive position;

- evaluating new business units with performance metrics used by mature businesses;
- making a wholesale bet on an unproven technology that may bankrupt the organization;
- assigning managers from mature businesses to lead new product initiatives in newly created business units.

Notes

1 Andy Grove, *Only the Paranoid Survive*, New York, 1997.
2 Clayton Christensen, *The Innovator's Dilemma*, Harvard Business School Press, Boston, MA, 1997.
3 See "Implanted Microchip Shows Promise in Delivering Drugs," *Wall Street Journal*, February 17, 2012, p. B1.
4 M. E. McGill and J. W. Slocum, Jr., "Unlearning the Organization," *Organizational Dynamics*, Summer 1992.
5 See "Penguin CEO Adjusts to E-Books but Sees Room for the Old," *Wall Street Journal*, May 9, 2011, p. B9.
6 See "Book Venture, Born of Change," *Wall Street Journal*, October 30, 2012, pp. B1, B2.
7 See "Xerox Chief Looks Beyond Photocopiers Toward Services," *Wall Street Journal*, June 13, 2011, p. B9.
8 See "P&G's Marketing Chief Looks to Go Digital," *Wall Street Journal*, March 14, 2012, p. B7.
9 See "National Geographic Explores Digital Future," *Wall Street Journal*, April 4, 2012, p. B7.
10 See "Fujifilm Thrived by Changing Focus," *Wall Street Journal*, January 20, 2012, p. B5.
11 See "The Anti-Kodak: How a U.S. Firm Innovates and Thrives," *Wall Street Journal*, January 13, 2012, pp. B1, B4.
12 See "Drug Makers Refill Parched Pipelines," *Wall Street Journal*, July 11, 2011, pp. A1, A12.
13 See "Pfizer's Future: The Niche Blockbuster," *Wall Street Journal*, August 20, 2011, pp. B1, B2.
14 See "Merck, Pfizer Diverge on R&D," *Wall Street Journal*, February 4, 2011, p. B4. Also see "Rallying Pharma's Rebels," *Forbes*, August 22, 2011, pp. 95–97.
15 See "Intel Chips to Power Down," *Wall Street Journal*, May 18, 2011, p. B4.
16 See "Intel Rethinks Chip's Building Blocks," *Wall Street Journal*, May 5, 2011, p. B3.
17 See "Intel Tries to Crack Tablet Market," *Wall Street Journal*, April 11, 2011, p. B8.
18 Gary Hamel and C. K. Prahalad, *Competing for the Future*, Harvard Business School Press, Boston, MA, 1994.
19 "3M: Profile of an Innovative Company," Harvard Business School Case Study, 9–695-106.
20 See "Novo Nordisk's Medical Miracle," *Forbes*, February 28, 2011, pp. 78–82.
21 Ray Miles and Charles C. Snow, *Organizational Strategy, Structure and Process*, Stanford Business Classics, 2003.

22 See "GM Ventures Into Start-Ups," *Wall Street Journal*, June 14, 2011, p. B4.

23 See "Shrink It, Cure It," *Forbes*, January 17, 2011, pp. 80–83.

24 See "New Sony Chief Executive Reveals Fast-Forward Plans," *Wall Street Journal*, February 2, 2012, pp. A1, A10; also see "Sony's New CEO Vows to 'Revive' Company," *Wall Street Journal*, April 13, 2012, p. B4.

25 B. Nagyi and G. Tuff, "Managing Your Investment Portfolio," *Harvard Business Review*, May 2012, pp. 67–74.

INDEX

Figures and Tables are indicated by *italic page numbers*